IOWA STATE FAIR

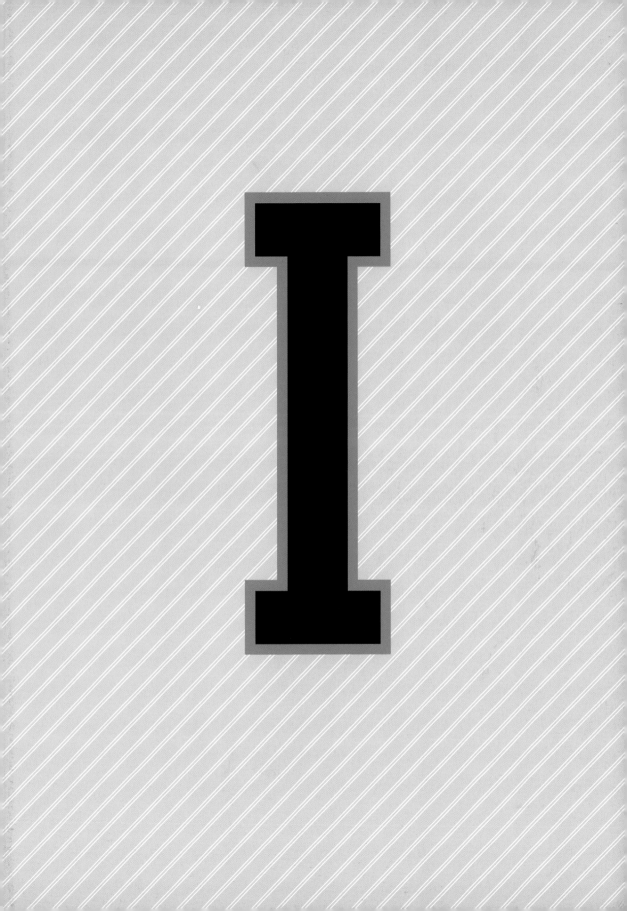

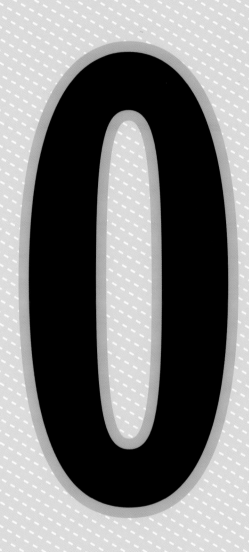

IOWA STATE FAIR

COUNTRY COMES TO TOWN

✳ ✳ ✳

Thomas Leslie

PRINCETON ARCHITECTURAL PRESS

NEW YORK

PUBLISHED BY
PRINCETON ARCHITECTURAL PRESS
37 EAST 7TH STREET, NEW YORK, NY 10003
WWW.PAPRESS.COM

FOR A CATALOG OF BOOKS PUBLISHED BY PRINCETON ARCHITECTURAL PRESS,
CALL TOLL-FREE 1.800.722.6657 OR VISIT WWW.PAPRESS.COM

DESIGN: PAUL WAGNER
COVER DESIGN: DEB WOOD AND PAUL WAGNER
EDITING: NANCY EKLUND LATER

SPECIAL THANKS TO NETTIE ALJIAN, SARA BADER, DOROTHY BALL, NICOLA
BEDNAREK, JANET BEHNING, BECCA CASBON, PENNY CHU, RUSSELL FERNANDEZ,
PETE FITZPATRICK, WENDY FULLER, JAN HAUX, CLARE JACOBSON, JOHN KING,
LINDA LEE, KATHARINE MYERS, LAUREN NELSON PACKARD, JENNIFER THOMPSON,
ARNOUD VERHAEGHE, AND JOE WESTON OF PRINCETON ARCHITECTURAL PRESS.
—KEVIN C. LIPPERT, PUBLISHER

PRINTED AND BOUND IN CHINA

LIBRARY OF CONGRESS CATALOGING-IN-PUBLICATION DATA
LESLIE, THOMAS, 1967–
    IOWA STATE FAIR : COUNTRY COMES TO TOWN /
THOMAS LESLIE.—1ST ED.
    P.   CM.
INCLUDES BIBLIOGRAPHICAL REFERENCES.
ISBN 1-56898-568-1 (ALK. PAPER)
1. IOWA STATE FAIR—HISTORY. 2. AGRICULTURAL EXHIBITIONS—IOWA—HISTORY.
I. TITLE.
    S555.I8L47 2007
    630.74'77758—DC22
                                    2007002169

Contents

HOTTEST TEMPERATURE DURING THE FAIR:
108°F
(OLDER IOWANS' DAY, 1983)

Receipts from 1st fair (1854):
$1,000
Receipts from 150th fair (2004):
$12,000,000

HOURLY CAPACITY
OF EACH SKYGLIDER CABLE
CAR ROUTE:
1,000 PASSENGERS

Number of parking spaces
in main lot:
8,000

Number of underage smokers
CITED AND FINED AT 2000 FAIR:
128

"This fair is such
a classic fair, where
others tend to
be more like
amusement parks"
—Garrison Keillor, 2005.

HIGHEST
ATTENDANCE:
1,053,978
(2004)

Iowa Residents polled
who have never attended a fair:
26%

"IOWA is hip
and fun:
the perfect little bit of
Americana."
—PRISCILLA TOTTEN,
TRAVEL EDITOR, USA TODAY

REASON GIVEN BY FIRST TIME
GRAND CHAMPION FIDDLER
NYALS PIERCE, 83,
FOR NOT COMPETING IN THE
EVENT PREVIOUSLY:
"DES MOINES' TRAFFIC"

TEN DAYS IN AUGUST

FOR OVER 150 YEARS, Iowans have come together for ten days every summer at the state fairgrounds in Des Moines to watch livestock competitions, stock car races, pie judging, and horse shows while eating corn dogs, cotton candy, and other foods served on a stick. The Iowa State Fair is an annual town meeting, classroom, and entertainment district rolled into one: the most important social event in the state each summer. One third of Iowa's population attends the fair each year, and although other fairs (in Texas and California) can boast of greater total attendance, no other agricultural event in North America matches the importance of Iowa's fair to its home state's economy, its social life, and its culture.

That such an event has maintained its importance to life in Iowa even as the state's demographics have changed is one of several contradictions inherent to the fair. Much of its appeal is nostalgic—a tangible link to an agrarian past that most Iowans have been disconnected from for a generation or more. But the fair is also relentlessly progressive, providing a forum for the dissemination of new farming technologies and agricultural methods since the first fair in 1854. Although the fair's major themes relate to agriculture and rural life, the event itself takes place in the midst of Des Moines, a metropolitan area of nearly half a million. Its exhibitors are almost all from the hinterlands, although its attendees

PREVIOUS PAGES

LEFT: From midway rides to corn dog stands, the fairgrounds are full of mobile architecture that is technically sophisticated and visually compelling.

RIGHT: Agriculture and Midwestern glamour collide at a goat milking exhibit about 1984.

[17]

represent Iowa's split between rural and urban residents. For most visitors from Des Moines, the fair is the one time each year they come face to face with the state's primary industries, and polite friction between city and country underlies almost every event and space at the fair. Likewise, the fairgrounds include camping for thousands of exhibitors and visitors, creating what annually becomes the tenth largest city in Iowa, on Des Moines's east side. This instant city of farm families stands in sharp contrast to the daily parking lots full of visitors from the suburbs, most of them in cars that would likely not survive winter in Iowa's rural areas.

These contradictions reflect the unique aspects of Iowa's population and geography. No state in the U.S. is more heavily tilled: more than 91 percent of Iowa's land is given over to mass agriculture, which is becoming increasingly industrialized.[1] Iowa's population is rapidly becoming more and more urban. More than 60 percent of the state's population is now metropolitan, while small towns continue to age out of existence. Yet Iowa's popular image is one of iconic, gently scaled landscapes, usually painted by native son Grant Wood, evoking a carefree, pastoral lifestyle. It is appropriate, then, that the fair highlights the contrasts between Des Moines and the countryside, as these two places and their ways of life have struggled to coexist throughout Iowa's history.

No one attending the fair, however, is likely to see it as the residue of such a struggle. The state fair is, simply, the best way to spend a hot August day in Iowa. The state takes these ten days off, right before school starts, during the lull in the growing season between planting and harvesting. Life in Iowa is tied to its cold winters, ecstatic springs, and foreboding autumns, and the heat of late summer matches the strolling pace and shaded lanes of the fairgrounds. If its tone is nostalgic—even elegiac—the state fair is nevertheless a connection to an agricultural history that for a week and a half becomes tangible, a reminder that Iowa's economy relies on the dirt beneath us and that not every tradition that has sustained rural life in the state has evaporated.

OPPOSITE

TOP LEFT: The Skyride offers panoramic views of the fairgrounds, including the Midway and Heritage Village.

TOP RIGHT: Alongside the classically inspired animal barns are hundreds of temporary structures, many with surprising architectural character of their own.

BOTTOM: Although the fairgrounds houses one of Iowa's most important collections of early twentieth-century architecture, the event transcends its setting, and the arrival of one million fairgoers each year transforms its acreage into one of the Midwest's greatest spectacles.

The hold the fair has on the state's collective imagination remains pow-
erful, and it has become a touchstone throughout the country for the
largely lost connection to our agrarian past.

* * *

Agricultural fairs in America date to the 1820s, part of an industrial
education movement that sought to build scientific principles into all
types of labor and production. By the middle of the nineteenth century, statewide fairs took place throughout New England, and their
progressive educational ideals and social attraction made them appeal-
ing undertakings for large farming states on America's frontier. Fairs
worked by disseminating information in the form of lectures, exhibits,
and demonstrations of new farming techniques and products, and by
hosting competitions that provided grading standards and comparative
opportunities for livestock and produce. Eventually, competition at agricultural fairs spread beyond the products of agriculture, encompassing
the arts and crafts of the home as well as the labors of the field.

Although Iowa was a relative latecomer to the fair movement, its
unique geography and history made it a natural locale for what would
become the greatest example of the type. Initially designated Indian territory, Iowa's borders opened in 1833, leading to a massive migration
of farm families seeking cheap land. Within three years, "Iowa fever"
had brought over ten thousand new settlers across the Mississippi River;
that figure would quadruple by 1840. Statehood was granted in 1846, by
which time Iowa's population was over one hundred thousand. Chicago,
settled only in 1835, became the prime economic force behind the
region's growth: Iowa's grain and eventually its livestock were shipped
there via a network of rivers; the Illinois and Michigan Canal, which
opened in 1848; and the railroad that reached the Mississippi by 1854.

Popular accounts have focused on wagon trains heading to points
farther west. But by far the majority of covered wagons stopped, sen-
sibly, in Iowa, where land could be paced off in 320-acre increments,

OPPOSITE

TOP: Iowa's largest
structure when built, the
Grandstand remains the
fair's most visible building, playing host to rock
concerts, country music
hoedowns, auto and horse
races, and even motorcycle
polo during its lifetime.
Its construction between
1907 and 1927 paralleled
the expansion of the state
during Iowa's greatest
period of economic growth.

MIDDLE: In 1902, the
newly solvent Fair Board
celebrated the new century
with its first major
permanent brick structure:
the Livestock Pavilion.
For more than one hundred
years, it has served as the
heart of the fairgrounds and
the fair's most recognized
architectural icon.

BOTTOM: The oldest
surviving structure at the
fair, Pioneer Hall (1884)
originally served as
"Floral Hall." Its timber
construction and
"Carpenter Gothic" detailing set it apart from the
fairgrounds' twentieth-
century structures.

where trees could be cut to build homes and farms, and where the soil's remarkable fecundity proved itself in harvests year after year.

Although farming was good in the early nineteenth century, Iowa did not offer an easy life. Travel was particularly difficult, as roads were almost non-existent until the 1850s. Farming remained back-breaking work, with implements and techniques having changed little, as one commentator noted, since Biblical times. Oxen-drawn plows were still used to break up the prairie and turn the earth, seeds were still sown by hand, and harvests were still cut and collected by scythe and cradle. Grain was ground by hand, using heavy millstones that had to be transported by wagon from suppliers on the Mississippi. Although McCormick reapers were factory-produced in Chicago beginning in 1847, it was not until the weighty implements could be carried by rail across the Mississippi that this new technology changed farming in Iowa.

Nevertheless, perhaps because of the inherent self-motivation of the state's first settlers, Iowa in its early days was relentlessly progressive both socially and technologically, serving as a conduit on the Underground Railroad from Missouri and establishing educational institutions ranging from one-room schoolhouses to colleges. By 1870, the state led the nation in literacy, despite its overwhelmingly rural nature. Advances in agricultural technology and techniques percolated throughout the state via county-wide fairs and colleges (Iowa was the first state to take advantage of the Morrill Act by constructing, in the 1860s, a land grant university.) This statewide belief in education was paired with a formalization of social events, necessary in a region where farms were often located a mile or more from their nearest neighbor. Although towns and even small cities sprung up along the Mississippi River, the progress of even the most rudimentary urbanization only gained speed with the building of railroads.

Collectively, therefore, Iowa's agricultural body—represented by everyone from farmers to wholesalers—recognized the need for an

OPPOSITE

TOP LEFT AND RIGHT: Advances in plowing equipment, planting techniques, soil management, and animal husbandry were traditionally disseminated through magazines and journals. By 1850 county fairs, which provided opportunities for lectures and competitions, began to raise the standard of agricultural knowledge while also allowing some degree of social interaction between farming families.

BOTTOM: When built, the fair's animal barns were some of the largest agricultural structures in the world. Their airy roofs and open side walls act as a sophisticated ventilation system, necessary when one thousand pigs come together during the hottest month of the year.

New Horse Barns, Iowa State
Fair Grounds,
Des Moines, Ia.

annual event that would disseminate the latest technology while offering an opportunity for a shared, statewide social occasion. The growth
of the county fair movement in Iowa from 1846 to 1853 set the stage
for an annual event that would come to both enlighten and amuse for
over a century and a half; how it balanced its educational purpose with
its status as the state's premiere entertainment venue would become a
long-running tale that would match the state's development and economic growth.

OPPOSITE

TOP: The fair's pioneering
days were celebrated with
recreations of nineteenth-
century farm life at the
1954 centennial fair.

BOTTOM: This aerial view
from 1967 shows the
Grandstand and parking in
the foreground and animal
barns to the rear. Except for
the reconstruction of the
old Machinery Building
behind the Grandstand, the
fair's buildings and grounds
have remained largely
unchanged since 1950.

CORN DOG

2 QUARTS FRYING OIL

2 CUPS FLOUR

1-1/3 CUP YELLOW CORNMEAL

1/2 CUP SUGAR

3 CUPS BAKING POWDER

2 TEASPOONS SALT

4 TABLESPOONS BACON FAT

2 EGGS

2-1/2 CUPS BUTTERMILK

1 TEASPOON BAKING SODA

24 HOT DOGS & STICKS

Heat oil in deep fryer to 370° F. Mix flour, cornmeal,
baking powder, sugar, and salt.

—

Add egg, buttermilk, and baking soda and mix until fully blended.
Prepare hot dogs by drying with paper towels and
inserting sticks.

—

Dip each hot dog in batter and deep fry until golden brown.
Serve with cheap mustard on paper towels
or paper plates.

✳ ✳ ✳

"THEY GAVE A PRIZE TO THE LAST ENGINEER TO JUMP OUT BEFORE THEY HIT: IT REALLY ADDED TO THE EXCITEMENT."

—FLOYD DEETS, 79, RECALLING THE 1932 LOCOMOTIVE COLLISION

Dumbest question asked "Domino Dan" Beckerleg each fair day:

"Are you going to knock those down?"

Maximum speed of "Skyscraper" crane ride:

70 mph

HIGHEST GROSSING GRANDSTAND STAGE SHOW

KID ROCK, 2004

$333,333

IN ONE SHOW

LONGEST

motorcycle jump at a Fair thrill show:

180 ft.

(ROBBIE KNIEVEL, 1995)

Number of dominoes

knocked down daily by domino toppler DAN BECKERLEG:

5000

"Mom doesn't watch."

—Lee Scroggins, Linden, Iowa on daredevil shows

"Number one, it's a business, and number two, every single person that walks up to the game isn't a winner."

—NICK VISCOMI, MIDWAY CONCESSIONS GENERAL MANAGER

BEST ATTENDED GRANDSTAND STAGE SHOW:

Sonny & Cher

(1972, 26,200 IN TWO SHOWS)

"ALL OF THE MIDWAY GAMES **ARE LEGIT.**"

—DAVID WERNING, IOWA DEPARTMENT OF INSPECTIONS AND APPEALS

CHAPTER ONE

THE FIRST FAIRS

IOWA IN 1850 WAS POISED between settlement and wilderness. Major towns such as Burlington, Clinton, and Dubuque had grown alongside the Mississippi River, while pioneer settlers had moved West through the state's river valleys. There, they found soil of unimaginable richness, left in a deep, loamy layer by retreating glaciers in the last ice age. With large tracts of land by necessity separating the farmers, agricultural life was predominantly solitary. Towns and mercantile centers sprang up throughout eastern Iowa, but the majority of the state's population remained isolated, with few opportunities for social or civic interaction.

Not surprisingly, then, much of Iowa took to the new agricultural fair movement of the mid-nineteenth century. Counties throughout the eastern third of the state formed agricultural societies that met regularly to share information, educate their members, and organize annual meetings. All of these fairs were centered around competitions, with high premiums awarded to the best examples of livestock, poultry, a variety of grains and plants, and industrial and domestic arts. By setting standards for animal breeding and handicrafts, the societies aimed to raise the quality of Iowa's produce and manufacturing generally. They predicted that the opportunity for farmers, mechanics, and artisans to compare their work with one another, and to compete against a set of objective

PREVIOUS PAGES

LEFT: The Grand Avenue promenade as it appears today is shown with the Des Moines skyline in the background. Each day of the event, the fairgrounds become the third largest city in the state.

RIGHT: The Grand Avenue promenade in earlier days.

standards, would provoke self-assessment and a general quest for the best methods and practices on the farm, in the shop, and at home. And they predicted right.

* * *

Jefferson County formed the first county agricultural society in Iowa, in 1852. Six other societies were founded in the same year.[1] The fair movement gained momentum in 1853, when the State General Assembly agreed to subsidize county agricultural societies. As many of these societies organized fairs were open only to county residents, calls soon went out for a larger event with a broader mission—one that would bring together farmers and residents from all over the state. In particular, articles in the *Iowa Farmer and Horticulturist*, a short-lived, progressive journal run by two agriculturists from Burlington, agitated for a statewide society and fair, alongside pieces on judging cattle and raising fruit crops. In June 1853, its editors proposed a meeting of parties interested in forming a state-wide organization.[2] The Jefferson County Agricultural Society took the lead, hosting a meeting at their annual county fair, followed by a formal meeting of representatives from other counties. On December 28, 1853, a group of delegates convened at Fairfield, the site of Jefferson County's annual fair. They established the State Agricultural Society and determined that the first annual Iowa State Fair should be held in Fairfield (then located in the center of the state's population), in October of 1854.[3]

To entice potential entrants and visitors, the state society published a preliminary premium list in July 1854 offering awards in thirty-three classes. In addition to prizes for cattle, horses, pigs, sheep, grains, fruits, and vegetables, premiums were offered in a class called "Inventions &c," which included items such as the best drawing of cattle, the best lot of pressed brick, and the best method for improving the roofs on houses.[4] Accompanying the release of the premium list appeared an open

OPPOSITE

TOP: The placement of the racetrack next to livestock competition tents and agricultural technology exhibits underscored the fair's ambivalence about its role as entertainment in 1854.

BOTTOM: Youth livestock contests have been a fixture at the fair since the 1910s.

1854

invitation to the entire state to participate in the fair, extended by the society's first president, Thomas W. Claggett.

> Let every farmer in the state and friend of agriculture who desires to see this great interest advance, consider himself as specially interested in this matter; leave not to others what is your duty to do yourselves.... Bring something, the best you have and compare it with other articles of the same kind. In this way you will see the defects in your own, and it will stimulate you to make more exertion in the future.... Come then friends to the Fair with your wives and daughters, and bring with each of you something for exhibition; do not fear that some one will have a better article than yourself, and that you will not obtain the prize, when it is not the money you want, but that you are actuated by the purer motive to encourage the great enterprise, and make our beautiful young state what nature has intended her to be, the garden spot of America.[5]

With its nod to self-improvement and the benefits of competition, Claggett's invitation suited the higher aspirations of the society well. The organization planned an event of the utmost sobriety, with a keynote address by a "distinguished stranger on the subject of Agriculture" and an appearance by "one of the most distinguished men in America."[6]

The fair that opened on 25 October, 1854, was almost entirely devoted to Claggett's stern call for objective judging of Iowa's goods. After the apparently unplanned (and therefore somewhat awkward) opening presentation of a gargantuan Danish cheese to the state's governor-elect and a parade of fair marshals, seven to ten thousand attendees watched reviews and exhibitions of livestock, farm equipment, poultry, and produce held on the six-acre fairground. The fenced-in perimeter lined with stalls and the 250-foot-long grandstand could barely accommodate attendees, nor could the surrounding town of Fairfield, whose hotels filled so rapidly that local homeowners were pressed to open their doors to strangers.[7]

Judging of animals and machinery occupied the first day, with displays of new plows and reapers taking center stage. Transportation being difficult, there were far more entries for horses and cattle than for less mobile swine. However, according to the organizers, the overall display of Iowa's crops and stock was "far superior to the best expectations."[8]

The fair's second day was given over to "domestic manufactures" in a specially conceived "Ladies' Department." In addition to knitting, quilting, baking, and stitchery, other arts were displayed, including the work of an early daguerreotypist from Dubuque. Also on the second day, the sole scheduled entertainment was held, which set the tone for a far less rarefied side of the fair that would continue throughout its history. The immensely popular but quite controversial display of "female equestrianism" had its start in an anonymous letter to the *Iowa Farmer* two months before the fair. The correspondent, "Laura," noted that the Ohio State Fair had offered a gold watch to "the boldest and most graceful Female Equestrian on the ground." A "quite spirited" contest had ensued, a "spectacle" that was hailed "the most attractive feature of the whole Fair." In the prim atmosphere of frontier Iowa, such a public display was unheard of and thus the earmark of an important, if salacious, attraction. Recognizing the potential boon for attendance but claiming rather to have based his decision on "gallantry," President Claggett himself offered the premium of a gold watch to the "boldest and most graceful Female Equestrian in Iowa."[9]

Whoever the anonymous letter writer was—if, indeed, she even existed outside the minds of the Iowa Farmer's editorship—the equestrian event that closed the second day of the Fair drew such a frenzied crowd that organizers agreed to an impromptu encore on the final day of the 1854 Fair.[10] The ten entrants followed the strict instructions of the Fair Committee:

Each lady...accompanied by [a] cavalier, will ride once round the circle, when the cavalier will retire to the centre, keeping within convenient

distance of the lady to render any service she may require… Each lady, after the withdrawal of her cavalier, will be entitled to ride four times around the circle, at any speed she may choose. After completing the fourth circuit she will retire to the centre.[11]

The spectacle that followed attracted an enormous crowd, who watched displays of horse riding that were alternately prim and daring. The judges professed an inability to reach a conclusion, thus ensuring the repeat performance (to which admission was, not surprisingly, also charged). At the conclusion of the encore, they awarded first prize to a Ms. Turner, of Lee County, noting her "easy, self-possessed and most graceful" ride.[12] However, the crowd disagreed, and thirteen-year old Eliza Jane Hodges of Iowa City was hailed as the people's champion for her "fearfully swift" ride and daring tricks. Men in the audience quickly contributed more than $200 for the "mild, poor, and unlettered" girl, deposited in the form of a scholarship to the Female Seminary at Fairfield.

The controversy—engineered or not—over the female equestrian competition is one of the most storied tales of the early fairs, with historians disagreeing over the intentions of the judging committee and the largely male crowd.[13] The alleged dispute between the judges—who rewarded proper, controlled riding—and fairgoers—with their more sensational tastes—quickly rose to the surface in subsequent fairs as the higher educational and civic aspirations of the fair's organizers were matched by vastly popular side entertainments. The former gave the event its cachet, while the latter brought in paying customers. The balance between social and intellectual propriety and the baser tastes of the typical patron of the fare would play out in similar controversies throughout the fair's history.

No less telling is this event of women's roles at the fair and by extension women's lives in the new state. The first fair by its very schedule and layout segregated awards and events into clearly defined gender

OPPOSITE

Women's Equestrianism—the scandal of the first fair—proved enormously popular at the fair. It was the first of hundreds of events that would attract audiences broader than just self-improving farmers.

roles, with livestock and agricultural premiums won almost entirely by men and domestic premiums bestowed only on women. By presenting female equestrians, the (entirely male) Fair Board proved itself both patronizing and exploitative. It portrayed the event as an opportunity for "the fairer sex," yet gladly accepted admission from a mostly male crowd, possibly motivated by more than an appreciation of fine horsemanship. This, of course, reflected the norms of the day, in which women's roles were strictly codified. Wives and daughters may have been equal partners in maintaining farms on the frontier, but in social situations segregation was a matter of both morality and habit. Women's participation in the fair's contests would chart Iowa's changing social standards over the next 150 years.

As wildly successful as the first fair was, it failed to earn a profit, due in part to counterfeit money taken at the gate.[14] Benefactors realized the importance of the event to the state and to Fairfield and a second fair, improved and expanded, was scheduled for 1855 at the same location. The State Legislature offered financial assistance as well, in recognition of the economic benefits in disseminating information and promoting higher quality produce and livestock. After 1855, the fair moved every two years to a new location, in deference to populated centers and to the woeful state of transportation infrastructure in Iowa. With rail travel, attending the fair became easier for fairgoers, but in the early years they arrived by horseback, covered wagon, or by boat. These traveling fairs were all located in eastern Iowa—in Muscatine (1856–57), Burlington (1864–65), Clinton (1867–68), Cedar Rapids (1876–77), Iowa City (1860–61), Dubuque (1862–63), and Oskaloosa (1858–59).

The traveling fairs saw a gradual refinement in competition and facilities next to sideshows that generated continuous controversy and great interest. In addition to livestock and horticultural competitions, agricultural contests pitted farmers against one another in races to plow a quarter acre. By 1865, the fair had grown to fill a thirty-acre site at Burlington, with stalls for 500 cattle and horses as well as "several hundred pens for sheep and swine." Burlington also featured the largest indoor halls yet, three parallel buildings each 130 feet long by 30 feet wide for the display of "Fine Art, Industry, and the products of the orchard, the vineyard, garden and fireside." Again, however, the display buildings were overshadowed by popular entertainment: "A splendid half-mile track, fifty feet wide" surrounded by an amphitheater with fixed seating for three thousand was to "afford abundant opportunity for the trial of speed and endurance of horses."[15] Horse racing became a primary attraction, requiring that strict rules against gambling be posted by the 1870s. Female equestrians continued to provide both entertainment and controversy with the Board of Directors stepping in to the debate in 1856:

> [T]hough this feature in our State Agricultural Fair has its interest, it is one we do not approve. It is one step in the path the 'strong-minded women' of the age would lead their sex, and its tendency is to draw women away from that retiring delicacy of character, and gentleness of demeanor, which are her chiefest charms in every relation of life.[16]

Despite protestations, this enormously popular event continued with supporters citing its educational benefit and its encouragement of safe riding.

The Civil War altered the fair's schedule, but Iowa's remoteness from most hostilities meant that it was one of only three states to continue its annual event from 1861–65. Fair attendees were dramatically split between uban dwellers who arrived by train or steamboat and stayed in hotels, and farm families who arrived by covered wagon with livestock and provisions in tow. The latter were increasingly accommodated in campgrounds near the fair's site, arrangements that the Agricultural Society recommended to avoid high hotel prices and ease transportation worries:

The plan is to hitch up your teams, and put your families in the wagons, and enough provisions and feed to last till you return home. If you have a tent or can procure one, by all means bring it along; but if your party is not too large you can sleep in the covered wagon. Let several families in a neighborhood join in the excursion, and its novelty and adventures will afford a rich field of enjoyment... Above all it will cost you no more than to stay at home.... Do not be afraid to bring your wives and daughters. Parties having ladies in company will receive special consideration from the Superintendent of the camp.[17]

Iowa's gradual western settlement and the relocation of the state capital to Des Moines in 1855 suggested that the fair might be better located in a more central, fixed home. Rail lines reached Des Moines in 1867, and the center of population moved westward as rail service reached Council Bluffs. The fair was held in Cedar Rapids from 1871 to 1878, and then in 1879 it moved to Des Moines. Here it stayed on temporary grounds for several years, taking advantage of Des Moines' good rail connections to Minneapolis, Kansas City, Omaha, and Chicago. By 1883, a temporary grandstand seated 7000 with standing room for nearly 30,000, alongside barns for hundreds of cattle and horses. The fair was an institution, now drawing thousands of visitors from all corners of the state. No longer content with its nomadic status, the State Agricultural Society appealed to the legislature for funds to purchase a permanent lot in Des Moines, on which barns and a grandstand could be built. This money was slow in coming, but in 1884 the state offered to put up half of the proposed $100,000 purchase price, on the condition that Des Moines itself raise the remaining funds for needed improvements. The Agricultural Society purchased a plot of farmland two miles east of the state capitol in 1885; what had been Calvin Thornton's farm would become the most important 266 acres of land in Iowa agriculture and, eventually, the most celebrated fairgrounds in the nation.

Calvin Thornton's farm east
of Des Moines became the
fair's new home in 1885.

BARBEQUE SAUCE

8 SLICES OF BACON, CHOPPED

2 ONIONS, CHOPPED

6 TABLESPOONS SOY SAUCE

6 CLOVES GARLIC

4 POUNDS TOMATOES, PUREED

1/4 CUP CORN SYRUP

1 CUP MOLASSES

1/2 CUP BROWN SUGAR, PACKED

2 TABLESPOONS CHILI POWDER (USE A LOT!)

4 TABLESPOONS DRY MUSTARD

4 TEASPOONS PAPRIKA

1/4 TEASPOON CAYENNE PEPPER

1/2 TEASPOON CLOVES, GROUND

3 BAY LEAFS

3 TABLESPOONS SALT

Cook bacon and discard fat. Cook onions with bacon until soft.
Add remaining ingredients, boil, reduce heat and simmer for 1 hour.

*A major event each year at the fair is the barbeque cook-off, with closely
guarded sauce recipes capturing highly coveted prizes. When it comes
to barbeque, Kansas City is really a southern suburb of Iowa.
This recipe makes for a great sauce, spread on pork or beef ribs in the last
five minutes of grilling. But beware of any 'authentic' sauces that
start off with bottled ketchup or Coke.*

✶   ✶   ✶

TOTAL PURSE
FOR FAIR CHECKERS
TOURNAMENT:
$200

Year Iowa Dairy Sculptor
Duffy Lyon created
first butter cow:
1960

Winning toss in 2005
Cow-Chip Throwing
competition:
146 feet
(AUSTIN ARNOLD, RIVERSIDE)

Method of judging
BEST MULLET
contrast between
"Business" (front) and
"Party" (back)

RED HENTON, 84, RETIRED
FROM HORSESHOES:
"I DON'T HAVE MUCH MORE
TO PROVE."

AVERAGE WEIGHT OF BUTTER
USED IN LYON'S
BUTTER COW SCULPTURES:
550 POUNDS

"She's like the
Mother Teresa of Iowa."
—MARTI ANDERSON,
DES MOINES, ON DUFFY LYON,
BUTTER COW SCULPTOR

World record horseshoe performance:
175 RINGERS IN ONE GAME
set at 1965 fair by
RED HENTON, MAQUOKETA, IOWA

Newest division in
hairstyle competition:
"best mullet"

Other sculptures by
Duffy Lyon:
AMERICAN GOTHIC (1996)
THE LAST SUPPER (1999)
TIGER WOODS (2005)

CHAPTER TWO

A NEW HOME FOR THE FAIR

T HE IOWA STATE FAIR was first held on its permanent grounds in September 1886. The move to Des Moines had not been without controversy, as residents in the eastern half of the state had grown accustomed to the easy access and biennial game of chance that brought Iowa's largest economic event to one of its cities. However, by the 1880s Des Moines had proven itself an amiable host. Rail and road service had grown exponentially in the state, and the city's location at the crossroads of major lines to all points of the compass guaranteed Des Moines's position as the economic and cultural center of the state.[1]

The provision of permanent quarters for the fair involved the single largest construction job in the state's history. Sturdy wooden barns and exhibition halls required nearly a million board feet of lumber, and the fairgrounds employed a permanent labor force of 150 throughout the summer of 1886. "A small town has grown up," one reporter commented of the eve of the fair. Hinting at the tension between rural and city atmospheres already apparent, he noted that Des Moines, "has now all the appearance of a prosperous and booming village."[2]

The topography of the Calvin Thornton Farm and its location just east of Des Moines's center formed an ideal site for the fairgrounds. Grand Avenue, one of the city's prime thoroughfares, extended to the

PREVIOUS PAGES

LEFT: The Exposition Building dominated the fair's skyline in the late 1880s.

RIGHT: The Livestock Pavilion, built in 1902, has hosted countless head of cattle and their chaperones.

farm's western edge. From there, the front half of the land was dead flat: perfectly suited to the large display buildings that would come to occupy it. The eastern half of the property, however, was hilly, rising about 60 feet above the surrounding terrain. A single summit offered a commanding view of the grounds and of the city below—in particular, of the bright dome of the recently completed State Capitol building.

The State Agricultural Society chose this highest point for the fair's grandest building: the 10,000-square-foot Exposition Hall. Its architect, William F. Hackney, modeled the structure on the Crystal Palace, the magnificent exhibition hall designed by Joseph Paxton and constructed in glass and iron for the 1851 Universal Exposition on a site just outside of London. Executed in vertical board and batten siding similar to that used in cladding farm houses throughout the state, Hackney's hall would be by far the grandest structure the Iowa State Fair had ever seen.

The building was laid out as a Greek Cross, topped by a great octagonal lantern and peaked roof, with gallery space radiating out through 64-foot-wide wings. Each of these carried a ridged roof, giving the impression of, if not exactly a church, at least a building of almost religious dignity. More than four thousand ground-glass windows provided daylight to the exhibits. To either side of the Exposition Hall, two smaller pavilions repeated this basic layout on a smaller scale, providing space for grain, fruit, and floral displays. Each of these were capped with a shingled cupola and clad again with vertical board siding.

These three structures would stand at the summit of the fairgrounds for more than sixty years, capping the long vista from the main, western-most gate. Their scale and formal appearance, however, stood in sharp contrast to the cacophony of temporary buildings on the flats that flanked the fair's main street, an extension of Grand Avenue leading from the gate, up the shoulder of Exposition Hall's hill, and finally into the rolling hills of the campgrounds to the east. Once inside the gate, a wooden amphitheater opened onto the horse track, which occupied the northwest corner of the site. Nearly 100 yards long, this structure held

OPPOSITE

TOP: Crowning the hilly east side of the fairgrounds, the Exposition Building—a 10,000-square-foot timber hall that recalled London's Crystal Palace (in form if not in materials)—served as the fair's greatest symbol for over sixty years.

⸺

BOTTOM: The Exposition Building towered over Grand Avenue. It was, for many Iowans, the largest building they would ever see.

more than six thousand spectators. The half-mile track, 70 feet wide in the main stretches, quickly gained a reputation as "one of the finest and fastest tracks in the West."[3]

The amphitheater and racetrack complex turned its back on the stock barns and show rings to the south of the extended Grand Avenue, where twenty-nine wooden barns housed sheep, cattle, and swine. A dormitory for exhibitors bore an alarming resemblance to the livestock barns nearby. Farther east, the Power Hall provided space for the display of agricultural equipment, while smaller structures housed offices for the fair's secretary, president, and treasurer, and for their staff. Finally, at the site's southern edge, the Rock Island Railroad built a dedicated passenger depot, providing a direct connection to downtown Des Moines and to the railroad's home territory far to the east.

All of these wooden structures (save one) would be replaced over the coming century. The flats would see several barn arrangements in the ensuing decades, although their easy access from rail and road would ensure that they always housed livestock and machinery. Domestic crafts and produce remained in the hilltop buildings beyond World War II. The amphitheater would, in its three incarnations, continue to dominate the western half of the site, neatly calling attention to the sensationalist entertainment nestled among attractions dedicated to the purer callings of rural life. The fair that opened in 1886 occupied buildings that would nearly all outlive their usefulness, but one can recognize today's fair in its organization of the state's economy and daily life across the terrain of the fairgrounds: its basic divisions—domestic crafts, plant and animal farming, machinery, and spectacle—remain remarkably unchanged.

Filling in the gaps between large entertainment venues and temples to agriculture were dining halls and "amusements," with their tents, barker stands, and other temporary structures. Countless franchises were issued, including thirty "simple and plain" eating houses, along with half a dozen dedicated sideshows.[4] The largest of these was the famous Cyclorama of Gettysburg, a wrap-around painting depicting the Civil

OPPOSITE

TOP: Standard fair buildings in the nineteenth century were built of timber, often with vertical board siding, similar to the structures that farmers would see on a daily basis.

MIDDLE: The Exposition Building spoke to the fair's highest cultural aspirations, but the majority of the grounds were given over to stock barns, simple structures that housed livestock and their handlers in cramped and uncomfortable conditions.

BOTTOM: The fairgrounds felt very much like a chaotic village of timber and tents. The facilities would seem increasingly inadequate as the economic boom of the 1880s gained steam.

War battle both geographically and chronologically. Other sideshows were of more dubious value, despite the management's public claim that the "character" of all would be "closely guarded." Nevertheless, the fair satisfied its director of franchises' promise that there would be "plenty of chance for everyone to be amused and fed and instructed." Bolstered by an extra day's opening to compensate for a stretch of bad weather, the attendance record of the 1886 fair exceeded those of all previous years.

Despite this increased popularity and the relative permanence of its new home, the fair soon entered its most troubled fifteen-year period. Now attached to Des Moines and responsible for the upkeep of permanent buildings, the State Agricultural Society quickly found the Legislature's generosity spent: it had all been expended on the purchase of land.[5] The economic boom that had accompanied the state's expansion slowed by 1890. The de facto monopoly of Chicago meat-processing concerns drove down prices for live cattle, while the railroads conspired to drive up transportation costs, creating an artificial depression in cattle markets that brought ruinous conditions to western Iowa in particular.[6] Farmers formed alliances, which the society declared unwelcome at the fair. Meanwhile, Des Moines proved a fickle host and had to be persuaded to support the fair, both financially and in terms of attendance. The city inaugurated a parallel civic celebration—"Seni-Om-Sed"—in the 1880s, designed to support the fair as an added attraction. The carnival and parade distracted urban patrons, however, and contributed to declining revenues at the fair throughout the early 1890s.[7]

The Agricultural Society responded to these challenges by redoubling its efforts at entertaining the crowds. The Des Moines fairs of the era replaced the previous emphasis on agricultural education with a full-throttle embrace of the sensational. Although the number of animal exhibits increased, leading to continuous construction of new animal barns, horse racing and grandstand events outpaced their growth, with balloon ascensions, parachute jumps, and, in 1894, the spectacle of a human cannonball fired from a mid-air emplacement, suspended

OPPOSITE

As Des Moines grew and rail connections enabled Iowans from around the state to attend the fair, organizers appealed to both urban and rural audience with advertisement such as this one, for the 1894 fair.

by two hot-air balloons.[8] This "most thrilling novelty of the age" abandoned all pretense of edifying its audience.

Horse racing, with its attendant vices of gambling and liquor, soon became the most popular fair attraction for Des Moines residents, and as early as 1890 the local press clamored for more of the fast horses and less of the "old fogy customs" that appealed to the somewhat more sober contingent of farmers and their families.[9] The earlier debate over the propriety of female equestrianism was here turned up considerably, as the "conspicuous moral tone" of the fair met the titillation of toned acrobats and the temptations of easy money at the horse track.

As the fair's financial situation worsened during the depression years of 1893 through 1897, the Agricultural Society grew increasingly desperate. In 1896 it allowed one promoter to stage a head-on collision between derelict locomotives in the Grandstand. The promoter agreed to a fee equal to a percentage of the day's ticket receipts over the previous one-day record, a bold proposal that paid off handsomely.[10]

The fair suffered from the decade's large exhibitions, notably the 1893 Columbian Exposition in Chicago, which sapped attendance dramatically (despite a fireworks display in Des Moines designed to resemble "The Last Days of Pompeii"). Attendance became such a pressing issue that the Agricultural Society voted to suspend the fair in 1898, the year of the Trans-Continental Exposition in Omaha, rightly figuring that they could lose money just as well without going to the trouble of staging the actual event.[11]

Stunned by the collapse of the state's premier agricultural event, the State Legislature stepped in, declaring that "fairs are of inestimable benefit to the state." In 1900, the Legislature dissolved the State Agricultural Society and moved the fair under the auspices of the Department of Agriculture. Eventually, the fair was given its own governing board, and with the guarantee of state support it began a run of three profitable decades, during which it became self-sustaining.

With state oversight, the fairgrounds suddenly became a worthy

OPPOSITE

TOP: Fairgoers in 1900.

BOTTOM: The Fair Board was reduced to desperate measures during the economic depression of the late 1890s. Grandstand events became increasingly sensational in order to attract an urban crowd—the fair's mainstay in difficult times.

Thrilling Death Duel!

investment. The original timber buildings and barns were, by the time of the state takeover, in need of repair or replacement. The Department of Agriculture undertook a massive building campaign between 1900 and 1929 that redefined the look and scale of the fair. Its aspirations were high, and its choice of architectural style and construction methods reflected both a progressive attitude and a serious financial commitment. The new buildings, however, also codified the fair's essential dichotomy—an urban spectacle based on the economy and labor of the hinterland.

The "Midway" had been formally established in 1897, on leftover land just east of the race track. Here, whatever remaining strictures of taste, morality, and ethics that prevailed elsewhere on the grounds were cast aside. Thrill rides, games of dubious odds, and even burlesque shows (labeled, simply "Men Only") sprouted up, the heirs of the "amusements" of earlier times but with a rapacious economic bent and a decidedly sordid atmosphere. This precinct was based intentionally on the 1893 Columbian Exposition's Midway, a collection of unauthorized stalls, amusements, and less-than-pure entertainments that had sprung up between that fair's entrance and its rail connection to downtown Chicago.

In the more respectable agricultural pavilions built on the flats of the fairgrounds, an architectural compromise was struck that similarly reflected the paradoxes of the fair. In replacing timber barns for sheep, swine, cattle, and horses, and in reconstructing the grandstand, the fair's builders chose to employ a hybrid language. The new barns were built of steel and wood on the interiors, with roofs that allowed daylight to infiltrate stalls and showrings while encouraging the ventilation of foul air—a pragmatic, almost industrial formulation. On the exterior, however, these barns were dressed up, with Beaux-Arts-inspired brick skins, complete with ornament that emphasized formal entryways and centralized massing. Such a choice reflected the grand civic aspirations of the fair.

OPPOSITE

TOP: Inspired by the success of the unofficial amusements on the Midway of the 1893 Columbian Exposition in Chicago, Iowa State Fair's Midway was established in 1897. Offering thrill rides, (dubious) games of chance, and exotic displays ranging from the shocking to the merely tasteless, the Midway would become one of the fair's main attractions.

BOTTOM: Crowds at the fair in 1900 relax along Rock Island Avenue.

[57]

Brick was, at the time, an expensive material, available from kilns located throughout the state, but rarely used in agricultural settings, except, perhaps, for foundations. Timber would have been the more typical, and economical, choice, as barns and domestic structures throughout the state most often took advantage of Iowa's existing (but since, entirely depleted) forests. Des Moines, however, had by century's end a tradition of masonry and neoclassical architecture, particularly notable in the 1884 Iowa State Capitol building, a sumptuous interpretation of the style, and in the State Historical Memorial, an ersatz treatment completed in 1898. Des Moines and other urban areas in Iowa built in a consciously formal Beaux-Arts style between 1900 and 1930, posing programs of civic importance against the otherwise endless landscape of rural vernacular construction. The Department of Agriculture became one of the premier proponents of Iowan neoclassicism, choosing to dress the fair's animal barns and produce judging arenas in the architectural language of city and state government.

Although the actual junctions between external brick skin and internal iron shed are often awkward, the resulting character of buildings on the fairgrounds is surprisingly urbane—welcoming to sophisticated patrons from Des Moines while inherently dignifying of the agricultural events held within. Between 1902 and 1929, eight major exhibition structures were built on the western half of the grounds, setting the atmosphere and style of the fair that prevails to this day, while codifying the fair's values in brick, iron, timber, and concrete.

The 1901 fair would prove a financial success, finally eliminating the debts incurred during the 1890s and placing the event safely in the black.[12] But despite improvements to the fair buildings, the grounds remained a morass of mud or dirt, depending on the weather, and rumblings from the Des Moines press about their condition began in the midst of preparations that year. In particular, the *Iowa State Register* called for the creation on only of masonry buildings but of concrete sidewalks and roads paved in brick.[13] The *Register's* outrage at the

OPPOSITE

TOP: By 1900, elecricity had reach the Grand Avenue Concourse. This new technology enabled the fair to offer nighttime entertainments.

BOTTOM: The Agricultural Building was one of the major structures built at the fair during the early 1900s in the neoclassical style.

[58]

Visit the
Iowa State Fair & Exposition
Aug. 26th-Sept. 4th 1914

"shame" of the fairgrounds shared space with the paper's announcement that brick manufacture had become "Des Moines' Greatest Industry," and the paper's pages of advertising for brick and terra-cotta pipe suggests theirs may not have been a completely objective viewpoint.[14] Still, the *Register* kept up its campaign, noting at the close of the 1901 fair that that year's surplus of nearly $30,000 should be poured directly into improving the grounds.

There is a hint, here, of the conflict between city and country. Des Moines residents undoubtedly found the dirt roads and paths of the grounds more objectionable than most rural dwellers would have, and the call for paved streets was undoubtedly an attempt to "urbanize" the fair. The *Register*, however, noted that "roads with dust or mud three inches deep are not inviting to farmers or city people," and that improvements were needed if the fair were to expand throughout the new century.[15] Likewise, the dirt-floored, wood-framed exhibition buildings—"barns that would burn like tinder"—were seen as backwards compared to buildings in Des Moines, and the *Register* led the call for "exhibition halls worthy of the name...[built] of brick and steel."[16] The management of the fair, under the Department of Agriculture, responded immediately.

The new management embarked on a remarkable program of improvements and construction the day after the 1901 fair closed.[17] "Rock Island Avenue," the major promenade between the Rock Island rail depot to the south and the grandstand to the north, was paved in brick and concrete, "as solid and as smooth as stone."[18] Electric poles that had sprung up in the previous decade were culled to open up views along the fair's main thoroughfares. The grounds were tended throughout the summer of 1902 in order to eliminate the vast fields of unkempt weeds that had previously taken over the fair's open spaces.[19]

In the center of these improvements, the board constructed the Livestock Pavilion, the first major brick and steel structure on the fairgrounds. Designed to hold stock judging, lectures, and entertainments,

OPPOSITE

TOP: This view of the Livestock Pavilion under construction reveals its steel skeleton—a vast technical improvement over timber framing, which had dominated construction on the fairgrounds previously.

MIDDLE: The 1902 Livestock Pavilion heralded the dawn of a new era for the fair. Its vast scale and formal composition lent a new sense of dignity and importance to the events.

BOTTOM: The famous two-way entrance to the Livestock Pavilion allows animals and handlers to move in and out quickly and creates an impromptu staging area at the building's south end.

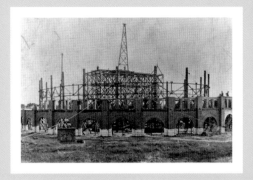

OPPOSITE
The Livestock Pavilion's
layout was as scientific as
its construction, offering
minimal obstructions and a
carefully laid out show ring
keyed to the walking gait of
cattle and horses.

ABOVE
The Livestock Pavilion was
dedicated, one day after
its official opening, at the
1902 fair.

the pavilion was a marvel for its day. Oval in plan, it boasted an enclosed clear span of 170 by 120 feet, with seating for nearly two thousand spectators. Tents and timber barns had previously held judging: the pavilion, with its immense scale and solidity, lent a sense of dignity to the proceedings. The pavilion was also a remarkably functional piece of architecture, with a three-tiered roof that allowed passive ventilation through clerestory windows and a perimeter of brick arches, trimmed in stone from quarries near Le Grand, Iowa, that could be filled by concessionaires. Fronting on the newly paved Rock Island Avenue, the pavilion became the new center of the fair, commanding views from throughout the flat western half of the grounds and rivaling the aging, timber exhibition hall on the hill for preeminence.[20]

The attraction of the newly paved roads and new-built pavilion, not to mention a restaging of the infamous "Last Days of Pompeii" in pyrotechnics, made the 1902 fair the most successful to date. Thousands of residents walked through the newly beautified grounds before the fair officially opened. At the pavilion's dedication (postponed due to rain on the fair's first day), laudatory speeches about its provision of shelter and comfort to residents from throughout the state marked the definitive change from the rough accommodations provided previously. Attendance on dedication day exceeded the previous daily record (which had been set on the day of the locomotive crash in 1896). Receipts for the week-long event surpassed $50,000, by far a record.[21] Encouraged by these figures, the State Legislature funded other large, capital projects over the ensuing years, each of which added urban amenities to the grounds.

The 1907 Agriculture Building was constructed at the fair's main crossroads, where the extended Grand Avenue crossed Rock Island Avenue. Located just north of the new Stock Pavilion and just west of the original wooden Exhibition Hall, the Agriculture Building was designed in brick and stone to be a permanent presence that would add a measure of respectability to exhibits. Set at an angle to both avenues, it

OPPOSITE

TOP: Following construction of the Livestock Pavilion, the Fair Board invested in a brick and timber structure at the intersection of Grand Avenue and Rock Island Avenue. The 1907 Agriculture Building has served as the center of agricultural displays ever since.

MIDDLE: The neoclassical composition of the Agriculture Building and its use of expensive stone and concrete detailing give some idea of the cultural aspirations held by the Fair Board for the annual event.

BOTTOM: Recently restored, the Agriculture Building still offers an encyclopedic collection of Iowa's crops and produce.

BIRDS EYE VIEW, IOWA STATE FAIR GROUNDS, DES MOINES, IOWA

featured a resolutely symmetrical, Beaux-Arts plan, with a cathedral-like arrangement of barrel-vaulted nave and transept. A pair of entry rotundas flanked the central bay on the long elevation. Inspired by the central exhibition halls of Chicago's Columbian Exposition, the Agriculture Building was a major statement about the cultural aspirations of the fair. Its monumental entries and imposing elevations suggested that the fair's rural functions were supplemented by a grander purpose, namely, the coming together of the state in its largest city for an event no longer simply economic or educational in nature. The design and construction of the Agriculture Building represented a statewide sense of the importance of the civic and social aspects of the fair. Dressed in a stripped-down, brick version of Chicago's White City, it lent an air of gravitas to the fair's major crossing point, putting the fair on par, stylistically, with the great Beaux-Arts libraries, civic centers, schools and institutions that were built in the neoclassical style during the era.

In fact, skins of brick and terra cotta composed in Beaux-Arts fashion formed the fundamental recipe for all but one of the fair buildings constructed over the coming decade. Along with the Agricultural Building, two new barns were built in 1907, for horses and swine. Although the Horse Barn was a fairly traditional gabled structure, the Swine Barn was a state-of-the-art agricultural building, with a scientifically derived roof profile that provided superior clerestory lighting and ventilation. Particularly on hot days, the Swine Barn's roof encouraged foul air to escape through long, open windows at roof level, drawing in air from the open exterior walls at the barn's perimeter. The roof covered 185,000 square feet of stalls, exhibitions, and two central show rings seating over eight hundred spectators. At the time of its construction, the Swine Barn was the largest agricultural structure in the world.

Three other major structures of the era repeated the combination of formal brick and stone exterior with a more functional metal and timber interior. The Machinery Building, finished in 1911, housed tractor and engine exhibitors on Grand Avenue, adjacent to the 1908 Administration

OPPOSITE

TOP: Produce displays take center stage in the Agriculture Building at the 1908 fair.

BOTTOM: The Agriculture Building's 'transept' was appropriately decked out in local grasses and grains for the 1910 fair.

ABOVE
The Administration Building,
known as "Iowa's Front
Porch," continues to serve
as the fair's hub.

OPPOSITE
TOP: The Horse Barns, built
in 1907, were expanded
throughout the twentieth
century.

MIDDLE: The Horse Barns
served as a backdrop to
cattle judging in the 1910s.

BOTTOM: The 1907 Swine
Barn was a masterpiece
of agricultural architecture.
At the time, it was the
largest livestock structure
in the world. Its multi-level
roof brings in ample
daylight while providing
shade and allowing foul air
to exit.

Horse Barns, State Fair Grounds,
Des Moines, Iowa.

Ring of Hereford Cattle, Iowa State Fair Grounds,
Des Moines, Iowa.

Building, a brick structure designed with sheltering porches and a familiar domestic massing. The Cattle Barn, which would eventually house over thirteen hundred head, was built in phases between 1914 and 1920, replicating the gabled arrangement of the Horse Barn, while the Sheep Barn, built in 1915 and expanded over the next twenty years, repeated the logic of the Swine Barn, with a multi-level ventilated roof and a open brick perimeter wall. Representing changing fashions, the Sheep Barn featured an extensive ornamental program, with terra-cotta lamb's heads staring down from the entrances, an eclectic set of entry pavilions, and a more visible clerestory roof. Although the ornament anticipated the rise of the art deco style, the strong roof planes are more domestic, an unusual mix that nonetheless created one of the fair's most architecturally consistent buildings.

By far the most visible artifact of the fair's most active building program is the Grandstand. By 1907 the popularity of horse racing and other spectacles began filling the timber seating on the south side of the main show ground beyond its capacity. Funds were raised in 1907 to replace that structure with something more substantial, but in a nod to the official priorities of the Agriculture Department that money was used instead for construction of the Swine Barn. The "crying need" for a larger grandstand for the fairgrounds was finally addressed in 1909, when an exposed steel structure seating six thousand was erected.[22] Although a large structure, it was dwarfed by the half-mile track it served. Built adjacent to the finish line on the front straightaway, the grandstand had a uniquely curved shape that allowed it also to function as concert seating. Uncovered stands provided additional seating. When the management of the 1909 fair opened the new grandstand, free of charge to the public, an overflow crowd of fifteen thousand filled the seats and grounds for a concert by Sig Liberati. That day shattered all attendance records, drawing twenty-seven thousand.[23]

In addition to record attendance, the 1909 fair also boasted the greatest capital expenditure. The grandstand had cost $150,000, and

OPPOSITE

TOP: The Swine Barn's metal roofs cover a variety of spaces, including pens, judging corrals, and exhibits.

MIDDLE: Built in stages between 1914 and 1920, the Cattle Barn features a sales pit in addition to its ranks of gabled stalls.

BOTTOM LEFT: By the time the Sheep Barn was constructed, architectural tastes had mellowed somewhat, moving away from the strict formality of the fairgrounds' first brick buildings. Extensive terra-cotta ornament livened up this new barn.

BOTTOM RIGHT: The renovated Varied Industries Building maintained the brick entry and corner pavilions of its predecessor, a nod to the building's heritage.

OPPOSITE
The original timber
grandstand hosted horse
races, seen by many as
vice-ridden and immoral,
around the turn of the
century.

ABOVE
By 1909, the condition
of the timber grandstand
(shown here) had
deteriorated. The Fair Board
made a bold commitment
of $150,000 to build a new,
steel grandstand.

with additional projects including the extension of the Cattle Barn the fair management spent over a quarter of a million dollars that year. By the time the Sheep Barn was completed in 1917, the capital program that the Board had embarked on in 1902 had completely remade the fair. Although timber structures remained scattered throughout the grounds, the event was now housed in permanent buildings of steel and brick. The atmosphere of the gathering had likewise changed. Gone were the mud paths, replaced by concrete and macadam streets. The fairgrounds now featured large, long-span structures, Beaux-Arts facades and electrified street lamps. The barns, moved off Grand Avenue to the southern end of the site, still contained livestock and produce raised in the hinterland, but they shared preeminence with events held in the Grandstand, as the fair catered more and more to residents of Des Moines. Alongside the new Sheep Barn, automotive spectacles such as races and "auto polo" made their debut at the Grandstand in 1917.[24]

Feats of aviation also became an important draw for the fair, for urban and country audiences alike. Balloon ascensions had been common since the 1890s, but the arrival of the lighter-than-air dirigible in 1906 created a sensation. Circling the fairgrounds and Capitol building, it brought activity below to a halt. A year later, a windstorm blew Roy Knabenshue's airship into electric light wires, igniting the mineral-oil soaked bag and dramatically precluding any flight—a harbinger of hard times to come. Crowds in 1907 were forced to made do with what may have been the nation's first tractor pull: a competition between two traction engines to plow sod while weighted down with twenty-two gang plows each.[25] But the flying machine retained its place at center stage. In 1914, ace pilot Eddie Rickenbacker attracted overflow crowds to the Granstand to witness a race between a car and his biplane. Aviation would enjoy a dramatic, if short-lived, reign as the supreme spectacle of the fair, and would come to play a key role in the success of the greatest fair of all time, held just before Iowa's darkest decades.

OPPOSITE

The fair expanded its offerings in the earlier 1900s to include spectacular aviation events, including the exhibition of a lighter-than-air dirigible in 1906, shown here circling the Iowa State Capitol.

OPPOSITE
Aviation found a home at
the Grandstand in the
1910s. Here, flying ace
Eddie Rickenbacker drives
against a piloted biplane
around the horse track.

ABOVE
The new steel Grandstand
attracted large crowds for
concerts and racing after
its construction in 1909.

[81]

PORK TENDERLOIN

Start with the best whole pork loin you can find and
cut it into 5–ounce steaks.

—

Run it through a tenderizer 3 times (or pound with a jacquard)
to put lots of little cuts in the meat.
Tenderizing the cutlet expands it to about softball size.

—

Dredge it through milk and then lay it into a bed of medium cracker meal.
Cover it with plenty of cracker meal and smash the meal
into the loin with your fist or the bottom of a bowl, making sure
it is completely covered with breading.

—

Deep fry in the finest vegetable oil you can find (Canola) at about 340° F.
The first few you cook will be fairly light colored; the more of them you cook,
the darker they will be.

—

Serve on a large corn-dusted Kaiser bun with all the fixins.

From Steve Fugate of the Hamburg Inn, Iowa City,
home of the Pie Shake, who respectfully points out that State Fair
tenderloins are actually frozen.

✦ ✦ ✦

AND MOST ECONOMICAL

"Half of fairgoers come for the food."
—PHIL SISSON, GRUNDY CENTER, IOWA

NUMBER OF CLASSIFICATIONS FOR FOOD ENTRIES: 900

Amount of batter mix consumed by one corn dog stand during the fair:
2000 lbs.

Pounds of pork chops
CONSUMED AT THE FAIR ANNUALLY:
6,000

"People go for low carb."
—Debra Weeks,
Meatballs-on-a-Stick vendor

NUMBER OF YEARS "LOW-FAT" CORN DOG WAS AVAILABLE AT THE FAIRGROUNDS: 1 (1999)

Miles of toilet paper used each fair:
1,700

"It's actually a rib chop with some of the meat taken off the rib so you can hang on to it."
—IOWA FIRST LADY CHRISTIE VILSACK, EXPLAINING LOGISTICS OF PORK-CHOP-ON-A-STICK

"ANYTHING YOU PUT ON A STICK USUALLY SELLS PRETTY GOOD."
—JEREMY CRUTCHFIELD, FAIR CONCESSIONAIRE

Fairgoers who ranked "CORN DOGS" their favorite food: 17%;
Fairgoers who ranked "BEER DOGS" their favorite "food": 20%

CHAPTER THREE

A FAIR FOR A NEW ERA

TTENDEES AT THE 1927 fair could well be forgiven for assuming that Des Moines and the fair had the brightest possible futures. The long economic boom of the early twentieth century had put Iowa squarely at the forefront of the richest agricultural region on earth. Automobiles had supplemented railroads in enabling transportation and commerce throughout the state, and new industries were supporting more efficient farming while creating a new economic base in the state. John Deere, for example, rose to prominence as the premier manufacturer of agricultural power, opening factories in the Quad Cities and Waterloo. New factories appeared in Des Moines, as well, and the working class that they gave rise to added to its booming financial market. All of this was based, of course, on farming, but the new efficiencies of scale and delivery meant that by 1927 Iowa was a state that was well off and able to afford an increasingly sophisticated cultural and social life. Grandstand acts at the state fair now alternated opera and classical performers with more popular fare.

Among the more important developments of the 1920s was the growing participation of youth in the fair's agricultural competitions. Both Future Farmers of America (FFA) and 4-H blossomed in the early decades of the century, underscoring the importance of education to rural youth. Special competitions were held for animals raised by

PREVIOUS PAGES
LEFT: Pigs made from lard celebrate the world's most economical shortening. The tradition of sculptures in unusual media continues today with the more appetizing butter cow.

RIGHT: The Administration Building's porch serves as the venue for hard-fought checkers tournaments.

[87]

club members (a tradition that continues today) and entertainment for farm children demonstrated a decidedly educational bent. Meanwhile, competitions for adults hosted by a newly resurgent Fine Arts department showcased the developing school of regional realism. Grant Wood, Iowa's greatest painter, received his first major recognition as the winner of the painting category several years in a row.

The economic growth of the state coincided with its greatest population boom, and attendance rose steadily at the fair during the 1920s. Weather permitting, each fair typically broke the previous year's attendance record, and by the mid-1920s the Grandstand proved inadequate for the growing crowds attending its horse races, concerts, and spectacles. In 1927, two major additions to the steel structure were built, extending covered the gentle curve of the original and adding covered seats to accommodate a total of ten thousand.[1] In addition, a new exterior was added to wrap the entire structure in a single, unified composition. Decorated with a military theme to commemorate the dead of World War I, the new exterior was the boldest statement yet of the fair's cultural aspirations. Designed to reflect the fair's other Beaux-Arts-style buildings, this wrapper consisted of repeated arches with a neoclassical frieze of windows above them, and two powerfully composed pavilions at either end, ornamented with terra cotta and brick. The spaces underneath the seating tier were refitted as exhibitions areas.

Nothing could be further from the rickety timber structure that originally occupied the site; but then, the fair itself had changed dramatically since 1890. The Grandstand was an urban monument above all else, and its new extensions and facilities meant that it could host events and racing throughout the summer—not just during the fair—for Des Moines residents. At the time, the 600-foot-long structure was the largest building in Iowa, and its impressive dimensions ensured that the fair's primary image was one of great scale and sophistication.

The Grandstand's reopening at the 1927 fair ensured a huge crowd, as did the perfectly rainless weather. The fair organizers chose John

OPPOSITE

Art exhibits in the 1930s took on an increasingly political tone as midwestern realism focused on the increasingly desperate lives of farmers and workers during the Great Depression, here depicted by painter Dan Rhodes.

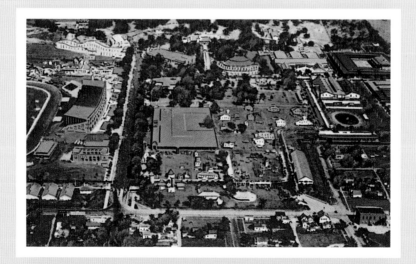

Philip Sousa's band to play the dedicatory concert, and attendance figures didn't falter for the interstate motorcycle polo match that followed the next day.[2] But there was an even greater attraction that year: Des Moines opened its municipal airfield the same week as the fair, and invited Charles Lindbergh to the dedication. Only a few months after his first transatlantic flight, Lindbergh was a phenomenon, and his presence in the City overshadowed everything else. Although frantic efforts were made to bring him to the fair, contractual disputes with his manager and with the city meant that fairgoers had to settle for a view of the *Spirit of St. Louis* circling several times over the fair, which came to a complete standstill.[3] In an attempt to cash in on the fever for all things aeronautical, organizers arranged for Ames native Clarence Chamberlin to attend with his aircraft instead, though his achievement as the *second* flier to solo the Atlantic did not draw the hoped-for crowds.

The fair's success continued through 1929, the event's Diamond Jubilee. In addition to hosting its usual attractions, the fair re-created exhibits, costumes, and scenes from the previous seventy-five years.[4] The city of Fairfield sponsored a full-scale reconstruction of the original state fair on the grounds. For the first time, events were broadcast live over radio throughout the state, providing a new marketing lure for Iowa's far-flung counties.[5]

The 1927 and 1929 events represented high-water marks in the history of the fair—marks that would not be equaled for a generation. Only a few weeks after the 1929 fair, the crash of the stock market signaled the end of the prosperity that had fueled the economic engines of the Midwest. Worse, Iowa was hit by severe droughts between 1930 and 1936, bringing social and economic progress to a sudden and terrible halt. The deprivations of life in the Iowa countryside during the Depression took standards of living back fifty years, and the fair could no longer celebrate the material and cultural gains of the state. By 1931, the fair was in debt again, and having so recently invested in infrastructure and building, it was faced with a grim situation, similar to the

OPPOSITE

TOP: The 1927 extension to the Grandstand included seating for ten thousand and a new, formal brick facade dedicated to the fallen soldiers of World War I.

MIDDLE LEFT: The Grandstand and Machinery Building frame the extended Grand Avenue and lend an urban scale to the fairgrounds.

MIDDLE RIGHT: The Midway is shown here in 1935 with the Grandstand in the foreground. Both the Exposition Building and the Women and Children's Building, visible in the upper right, would be demolished within a generation.

BOTTOM: This aerial view from the 1930s shows the animal barns, Grandstand, and Exposition Building. By 1929, all of the fairgrounds' major elements were in place. The structures and spaces of the fair have remained remarkably unchanged since then.

one it faced in the 1890s. Exhibits of machinery became perfunctory. Livestock shows diminished in number as healthy specimens became fewer and transport became financially impossible. As attendance plummeted, the fair reinstituted the locomotive crash in 1932, painting the two contenders with the names of that year's presidential candidates—"Roosevelt" and "Hoover"—to the delight of a deeply cynical crowd.

The locomotive crash marked the darkest year of the Great Depression in Iowa. An ill-fated farm strike in the western half of the state radicalized farmers throughout Iowa, and that year's fair saw unprecedented political discussion amongst attendees about the plight of the state and its agricultural economy. Although no further "farmer's holidays" occurred, the fair again saw political conflict in its beer tents and animal barns. As farmers suffered the droughts of 1934 and 1936, its agricultural displays withered. The fair was forced to intensify its urban appeal, staging pyrotechnic displays to draw urban crowds at night.[6] Nineteenth-century commentators who had been shocked by the spectacle of women's equestrianism would have been mortified by the gradual spread of burlesque tents throughout the Midway. "Girlie" shows had quietly been a part of the Midway tents since their inception in the 1890s, but burlesque became an essential part of the fair's appeal to men from city and country alike during the Depression.

Conflict between the lofty aspirations of the fair's organizers and the coarse offerings of the Midway reflected the broad, ongoing schism between the urban culture of Des Moines and the rural traditions of the countryside. In 1931, Des Moines native Phil Stong captured this tension in his novel *State Fair*. Although best known as the inspiration for the somewhat sunnier 1945 musical by Rodgers and Hammerstein, the novel itself is a surprisingly dark coming-of-age story that took as its major plot device the effects of the fair's worldly temptations on an Iowa farm family.[7]

State Fair tells the story of the Frakes, a family from the fictional town of Brunswick, who attend the fair with sure-fire blue ribbon

By the early 1930s, the optimism that accompanied the construction of the new Grandstand had evaporated. Fair organizers resorted to the sort of spectacle that had drawn crowds during the previous depression, of the 1890s, here restaging the infamous locomotive crash in 1932. Note the train's names.

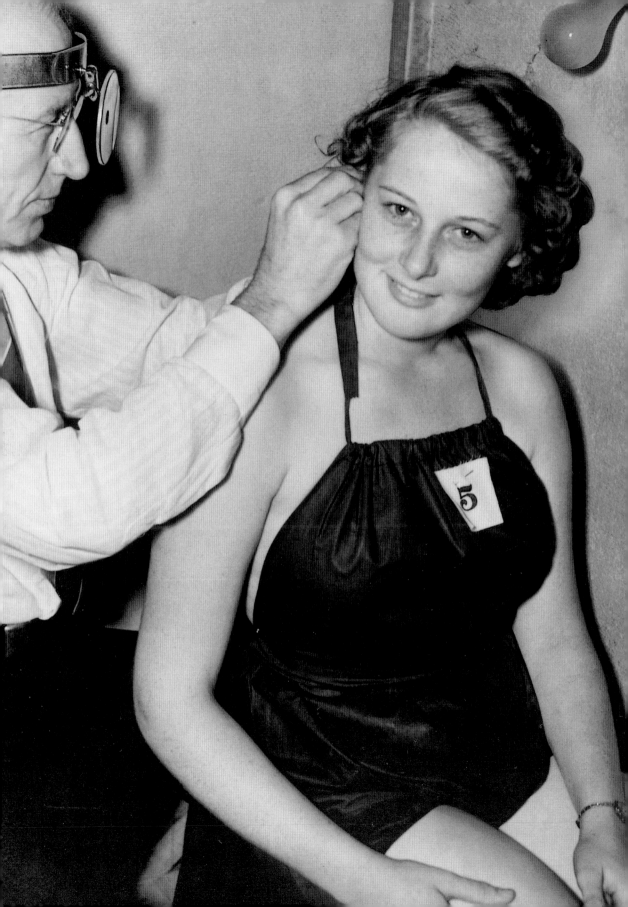

OPPOSITE

Human specimens were judged alongside their animal brethren throughout the 1930s, with prizes given for healthiest babies, boys, and girls. These contests' uncomfortable echo of eugenics led to their immediate cessation after World War II.

ABOVE

As the Great Depression worsened, the Fair Board turned a blind eye toward increasingly sensational—and racy—sideshow entertainments along the Midway, such as this "educational" sideshow exhibit from the late 1930s.

winners: a pig named Blue Boy and home-baked pies. While the parents attend to their pigs and pastries, the Frake children, both teenagers, seek out romantic adventures. The son encounters a brazen, worldly Des Moines woman (surely a literary first) who deeply unsettles his traditional values, while the daughter finds romance that is only as lasting as a transitory Midway ride. Although criticized for its sentimentality, *State Fair* nevertheless painted a remarkably bleak picture of relations between city and country folk in the state, with the Frakes returning to Brunswick, ribbons in hand, at once appalled and secretly thrilled by their urban experience. The novel memorialized the ideals of the fair, even as it exposes its artificial qualities; it suggested that the fairgrounds were a stage-set for false reconciliation between Iowa's cultures, although in fact its buildings themselves presented proof of the ultimate contradiction between the fair's agricultural and financial missions. A carnival barker who shamelessly defrauds the Frake boy serves throughout the book as a metaphor for a rapacious urban culture that viewed the countryside and its less-than-worldly citizens with contempt.

Other events of the era also served to underline the tensions between urban and rural cultures. Controversy over the fine arts displays had simmered since the 1920s, when longtime superintendent Charles Atherton Cumming rejected modern entries as primitive "jazz art" unworthy of inclusion.[8] The realism of Grant Wood's work had, for a time, provided a middle ground, easing the polarization of modernists and traditionalists, but the late 1930s ushered political themes into the formerly benign regionalist school. In 1938, the self-avowed "proletarian" theme of the winning painting, featuring two workmen carrying a ladder, was reviled by conservatives. Worse, its painter, Dan Rhodes, was commissioned by the WPA that same year to paint a mural in the Agricultural Building celebrating Iowa's centennial as an American territory. As with Wood's "American Gothic," reaction to the heroic but "hard-looking" Iowans in Rhodes's mural was mixed at best, and the mural's "vague" themes of liberty, connection to the land, and labor were largely lost on the

OPPOSITE
The 1945 Rodgers and Hammerstein musical *State Fair* presented a cleaned-up, sunnier version of Des Moines native Phil Stong's 1931 novel, which portrayed the tensions between urban and rural lifestyles as the inherent drama within the fair.

fair's attendees. Controversy erupted, however, when the press noticed that a key figure in the painting was sowing wheat with his left hand, an allegedly clear political symbol of both protest and communist leanings.

Political protest and artistic controversy were held at bay during World War II, as the fair shut down from 1942 to 1945. This was only the second time in its history that the fair had been cancelled; even the Civil War had not closed its gates. But the draft and the rationing of fuel sapped Iowans's ability to travel to Des Moines. The U.S. Army procured the fairgrounds as an encampment for the duration of the war. Barns that had housed livestock and swine now served as barracks, and the race track served as a parade ground.[9]

Just as the war created a definitive break between the America of the Depression and that of the postwar boom, the fair emerged from its hiatus as a distinctly different event. The years immediately following the war saw record attendance, particularly 1946, when it served as a celebration of the war's end and an unmistakable hallmark of Iowa's return to normal life. "If all the armies of the world had left as little change upon the scene of their activities as our army left upon the Iowa State Fair grounds," Wallace's Farmer remarked, "it wouldn't be such a bad old world after all."[10] Despite a lackluster showing of agricultural exhibits, that year's attendance—514,000—broke the half-million mark for the first time, and the fair turned a record profit.

Attendance declined, however, in each of the next five years, dipping back below the talismanic half-million mark.[11] Profits kept up, but interest in the fair during the postwar era began to falter. Iowa's changing demographics accounted for some of this, as its population continued an accelerating trend of urbanization, bringing greater access to cultural and social events. Likewise, the gradual spread of television in the 1950s brought entertainment and, eventually, education to Iowa's rural areas directly. The fair's central role in the life of the state was in jeopardy.

OPPOSITE

TOP: In this photograph from the late 1940s, from left to right along Grand Avenue are the Exposition Building (demolished in 1950), the Agricultural Building, the Grandstand, and the Machinery Pavilion. From front to back along Rock Island Avenue are the Agricultural Building, the Livestock Pavilion, the Cattle and Horse barns, and the Swine and Sheep barns.

BOTTOM: The fair in the postwar era had to contend with a more mobile population base, one that was increasingly distracted by travel and broadcast media. In response, the Grandstand brought in thrill shows and auto races.

[98]

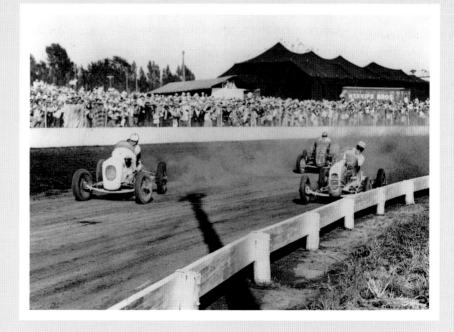

OPPOSITE

TOP: Although women's equestrian events had long since ceased to provide entertainment sensational enough for the fair's thrill seekers, organizers continued to seek out shows designed to keep visitors on the edges of their seats. Joie Chitwood's Auto Thrill Shows were a constant presence in the 1950s and 1960s.

⁓

MIDDLE LEFT: Judging of agricultural products— here in 1950—has always been a hallmark of the fair's educational, economic, and scientific mission.

⁓

MIDDLE RIGHT: Cold war exhibits included the Atomic Energy Commission's "The Atom and You," which allowed fairgoers to use robot arms to handle (fake) radioactive waste.

⁓

BOTTOM: A constant presence throughout the fair's history has been its campgrounds, an "instant city" in the hills to the east of the fairgrounds proper. Here, a family uses traditional methods to bathe in 1951.

Throughout the 1950s, the fair responded in two contradictory ways—by further tailoring its offerings to an increasingly urban crowd, and by marketing itself as a connection to the state's agrarian history. Grandstand entertainment in the postwar era focused on auto racing and popular musical acts. Increasingly sophisticated sprint and stock car races featured amateurs and professionals, and daredevil shows provided gruesome spectacles of crashes, leaps, and rolls. The Midway, meanwhile, continued to offer vices for all ages, from games of "skill" that always seemed to go badly to the burlesque tents that left their visitors with less cash and little reward. Although aerial displays were less common in the jet age than they had been before the war, new advances—a helicopter in 1951, for example—continued to attract the curious. Other cutting-edge technology took aviation's place. The Atomic Energy Commission was a regular exhibitor to the fair throughout the cold war, letting fairgoers use robotic arms to handle fake uranium in their "The Atom and You" display.

Alongside the grandstand attractions, the fair very consciously groomed its nostalgic image, and although this proved entirely successful, it belied its own progressive forward-looking origins, often in strange ways. At the 1954 Centennial fair, the event's heritage was the primary draw, resulting in a record year of attendance after nearly a decade of gradual decline. At the northern end of the grounds, the fair board again constructed a full-scale replica of the 1854 Fairfield fair, complete with historic agricultural implements and a horse track on which the events of the first fair were reenacted.[12] Female equestrianism caused less of a scandal in 1954, but the palpable difference in scope and scale of the present-day fair resonated powerfully. Inspired by the success of this look backwards, "Heritage Village" was constructed along the extended Grand Avenue over the next fifteen years. It featured structures from Iowa's past that were either moved from their original sites or reconstructed of the fairgrounds wholesale. Among the most popular exhibits were the Country School, originally built near

OPPOSITE

TOP: Heritage Village is the legacy of the 1954 Centennial Fair.

BOTTOM: The Agricultural Building continues to host produce displays, here in 1954.

ABOVE
The Midway overlooks the Grandstand and racing track, allowing a good view of the action on the first turn.

Indianola, and a replica of Iowa's "First Church," based on an 1834 log structure in Dubuque. Similarly, the sole remaining structure from the Thornton Farm was reopened as "Grandfather's Farm," hosting exhibits of historic agricultural techniques and machinery.

While looking to its past, however, the fair also dismantled some of its own heritage in its postwar evolution. Most notoriously, the board removed Dan Rhodes's WPA mural from the Agricultural Building in 1946, ostensibly because of its portrayal of Iowa farmers as "club-footed, coconut-headed, barrel-necked, and low-browed," according to fair secretary Lloyd Cunningham.[13] Those on the political left suspected other motives, but Cunningham pled ignorance of the mural's alleged symbolism. Pointing to economic concerns, he claimed that "plywood was expensive" and noted that the fair had also pressed into service a replica of Republican president Herbert Hoover's birthplace, as showers for the campground.[14] Whatever the rationale, 1946 spelled the end of politically charged social realism at the fair. The Fine Arts displays would henceforth adopt traditional standards of judging, penalizing paintings with any perceived social theme and favoring placid landscapes or agriculturally themed still lifes.

Of more import, but surprisingly less controversy, the fair Board tore down the original timber Exposition Building in January 1950, ending its lofty reign atop the western half of the grounds after sixty-four years. The Building had served the fair well, but its Victorian Gothic style was well out of touch with the rest of the fair's main structures and its timber construction was showing its age. The presence of a newly finished 4-H dormitory nearby was given as a reason, as the fire marshall expressed concern regarding the proximity of the two buildings.[15] In demolishing the Exposition Building, the fair board essentially trimmed the grounds' nostalgic image, eliminating the symbol of the previous century's difficult growth and leaving in place the brick barns, grandstand, and livestock pavilion as the fair's primary architectural icons. Although Heritage Village celebrated pioneer days, the

OPPOSITE

TOP: 4–H girls make up beds in the new dormitory, built in 1949.

BOTTOM: Despite the impact of World War II, the agricultural mission of the fair remained largely unchanged. This Hereford stays cool by using the only air conditioning available.

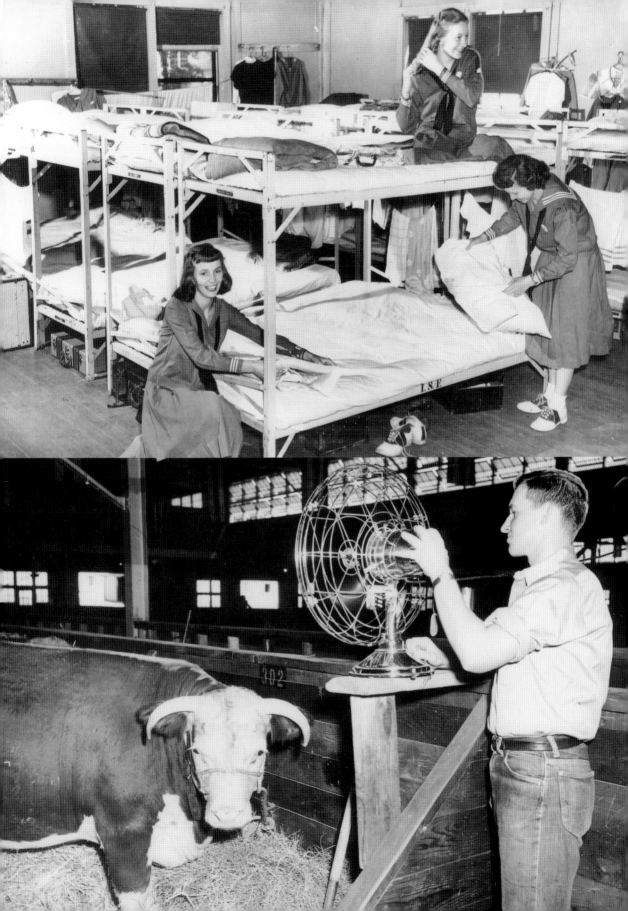

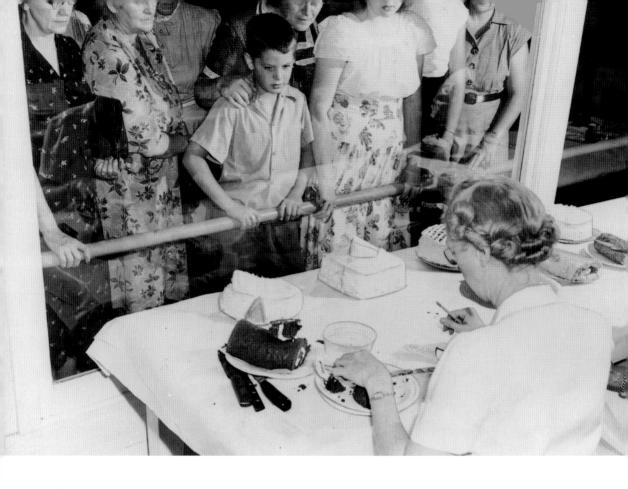

LL PURPO

...ER AND MOST ECONOMICAL SHORTENING

OPPOSITE
Cakes are Judged in 1948.
Consumer education
remained a primary focus
in the postwar era.

ABOVE
Among the more unique
traditions of the fair are
artworks carved from
agricultural products.
These pigs extolled the
benefits of lard in 1939.

larger structures maintained the fair's more progressive image. A single wooden exposition building—the old Floral Hall—was kept and restored as a monument to Des Moines's early, timbered era.

As the fair aged throughout the 1950s and 1960s, its popularity relied increasingly on its connections with an idealized agrarian past. Ironically, urban fairgoers began to report more and more that their reasons for attending were due less to the quality of the musical events or intensity of the thrill shows, and more to the sense of tradition that it represented. Such sentiments would have seemed bizarre only a generation before, when the fair was Iowan's primary opportunity to look forward: to developments in aeronautics and automobiles in addition to agriculture, education, and the growth of culture that Des Moines promised.

By the mid-1960s, however, the demographic changes wrought by the postwar economic boom propelled the state's evolution at an accelerated pace. Cities grew while rural towns emptied. Farms began to consolidate, and the population of the state became predominantly urban by 1960. If the early history of the fair reflected the growing move westward, the establishment of Des Moines, and the growth of transportation and economic links throughout the state, the story of the fair in the last half of the twentieth century was one of retrenchment, a struggle to define itself and its traditions against the increasingly mobile population that made up its base.

OPPOSITE

TOP: The fair's attraction for children has been a relatively recent phenomenon. Here, four young fairgoers and their charge check out the menu at a concession stand in 1946.

BOTTOM: Children's Day in the Grandstand is captured in this 1957 photograph. The demographic changes to the Iowan population in the late twentieth century has had a marked impact on the fair.

GRILLED CORN

12 EARS CORN

1 CUP MELTED BUTTER

SALT

Peel husks from corncobs, leaving enough just
enough husk to cover cob.

—

Brush butter onto each ear and
season with salt.

—

Re-wrap each ear with husks and aluminum foil.
Place over low fire for 25–30 minutes,
turning every five minutes.

Total annual entries in
prize categories:

54,600

Pounds of corn
per day consumed
by average
Grand Champion bull: 60

FATE OF GLADBROOK, IOWA,
HOG FARMER'S
COMPETITION BOARS:
**"They'll become
somebody's pepperoni
and sausage."**

Weight of "Skinny,"
2004 Super Bull contest winner:

2,996 lbs

NUMBER OF ALLEGED LIVESTOCK
COMPETITION CHEATING INCIDENTS
IN FAIR HISTORY: 1
*(THE "PICKLES"
INCIDENT, 2002)*

TOTAL ANIMALS ON
FAIRGROUNDS DURING FAIR WEEK:

16,000

Largest watermelon
on record:
118.8 POUNDS

TOTAL MANURE
PRODUCED DURING
FAIR WEEK:

2,000,000 lbs

Number of
BLUE RIBBONS
awarded annually:
30,000

NUMBER OF
**DEDICATED BARN
CLEANERS:**
FIFTY

CHAPTER FOUR

NEW TRADITIONS

ONCERNED THAT THE FAIR's agricultural focus would not hold its audience's attention against the popular culture of the time, the fair board embarked on a series of themed fairs during the 1960s. Attempting to replicate the success of the Centennial year, the fairs held between 1965 and 1969 each focused on a different era in Iowa's history, from the time of the region's habitation by Native Americans, to the period of settlement by farmers moving west, to the "Gay '90s" and "Roaring '20s."[1] After just five years, however, the fair board found itself struggling to maintain relevant themes and began to look farther afield for inspiration. The board chose "Discover Mexico" as its theme in 1971, complete with mariachi bands performing at the ribbon ceremonies.[2] The fair's thematic low point came in 1973 when "Discover Hawaii" brought luaus to the Grandstand and pineapples to the grilling contest. As the nation's bicentennial approached, American history took over: in 1974 "The Discoverers" paid tribute to Spanish and Portuguese explorers, and in 1975 "The Colonizers" featured English performers and exhibits. These fairs served as a perfect set-up for the 1976 fair, which diplomatically adopted the "Spirit of Iowa" as its focus.

Having exhausted state and national history, the fair's promoters abandoned themed fairs the following year, settling instead on catchy

PREVIOUS PAGES

LEFT: Despite this sign, fairgoers are advised to watch their step near the animal barns.

RIGHT: The fairgrounds' size is large enough to keep two lines of cable cars in constant action.

[115]

marketing slogans. The specter of floral shirts and hula dancers never darkened the fair's gates again.

The dalliance with themed fairs in the 1970s reflected fair organizers' insecurity in the era of improved educational opportunities and infrastructure. Exhibits were no longer the primary source of agricultural education in Iowa: universities had long since become the main conduit for information on new farming methods and technologies. Likewise, the social nexus that the fair had provided when transportation in the region was difficult became redundant with the completion of interstate highways. And with the advent of mass media, the fair now had to compete with television and new concert venues to attract its audience.

Throughout the 1960s, variety shows, patched together with available film or music stars, novelty acts, and musical dance numbers, dominated the Grandstand.[3] These shows catered to traditional audiences, and eventually organizers realized they would need to cater to popular tastes as well. They responded with a wide spectrum of concert offerings. The Osmond Brothers, Engelbert Humperdinck, and the Carpenters set a new standard for headliners, while country stars Tammy Wynette and Johnny Cash continued to draw "old-timers," as did Lawrence Welk, Red Skelton, and Tennessee Ernie Ford. Newer, younger acts such as the Jackson Five, the Fifth Dimension, and Elton John were soon added to the mix.[4] Disco made its appearance in 1979, as Chic headlined, while in 1985 Iowa teens set attendance records to see Tiffany and the New Kids on the Block.

Although youth from rural Iowa had long been served by a wide range of 4-H exhibition programs, the fair attempted to appeal to non-rural teenagers as well. In 1964 "Teen Town" promised "dancing to live combos, teen interest exhibits, autograph parties, hootenannies, [and a] teen queen contest," all held within a carefully monitored area. Teen Town guaranteed the fair's future with Iowa's baby-boom generation, giving the fair a cachet with the first Iowans to grow up as part of an urban majority.[5]

OPPOSITE

TOP: Johnny Cash headlined the Grandstand stage in 1970.

BOTTOM: Iowa is proud to be the spiritual home of sprint car racing, but amateurs compete in modified stock car racting as well, providing grandstand viewers with a range of entertainment.

ABOVE
In the 1980s fair organizers
mixed pop culture with
tradition. Here, fans line up
for New Kids on the Block
tickets in 1985.

OPPOSITE
This image, from *National
Geographic* in 1980, was
typical of the national
media's new-found interest
in the fair's elegiac
qualities.

[118]

The successful integration of urban spectacles with the fair's agri-culturally based traditions has been its mainstay for over a generation. Daytime at the fair is largely given over to agricultural competition, small concerts on the central "plaza," exhibits of farm machinery and a variety of commercial products (some, still, of legendary dubious-ness), in addition to the midway rides. Nights, however, focus on the Grandstand, where auto races alternate evenings with country and western, classic rock, and pop concerts. New traditions have sprung up since the 1970s, including the Bill Riley Talent Search, an all-comers competition, and the annual appearance of the Butter Cow, sculpted every year since 1960 by Toledo, Iowa, native Duffy Lyon.[6]

The fair's buildings began showing their age in the 1960s. Animal barns in particular, being unheated and open to the elements, fared poorly in the cold and snow of the off-season.[7] The fair authority brief-ly considered starting anew, as part of a master plan to provide entire-ly new facilities and a home for the World Food Prize, the agricultural equivalent of the Nobel, which is awarded in Des Moines each year. Such a move was quickly rejected, but routine maintenance was unable to keep up with the physical plant's deterioration.[8] By 1991, the needs had become acute, and the state formed the Blue Ribbon Foundation and charged it with fund raising for capital projects and restoration throughout the grounds. Iowans responded, and every major structure has since seen major repairs or renovations.

The foundation's work has emphasized the fair's connections to the past and, in particular, to family memories that date back several gen-erations. Iowans who relocated from the countryside to less rural areas feel a strong link to this annual event, which maintains agricultural tra-ditions. The foundation has capitalized on the fair's place in Iowa's col-lective memory.

Part of the foundation's campaign included the reconstruction of the Varied Industries Building, originally constructed in 1911 as the Machinery Pavilion. Beginning in 2000, the original, open structure

OPPOSITE

TOP LEFT: Politicians have long craved the wholesome atmosphere of the fair as a backdrop for their campaigns. Iowa's early presidential caucuses have helped to bring candidates to Des Moines each August, including Gerald Ford in 1975.

TOP RIGHT: The third-place winner in the "Best Looking Man at the Fair" shows off proof of his achievement in 1986.

BOTTOM: Amateur contests have long drawn Iowans from all backgrounds to compete against one another. The cow-chip throwing contest (featured here) regularly takes place alongside the husband calling and ladies' nail driving contests.

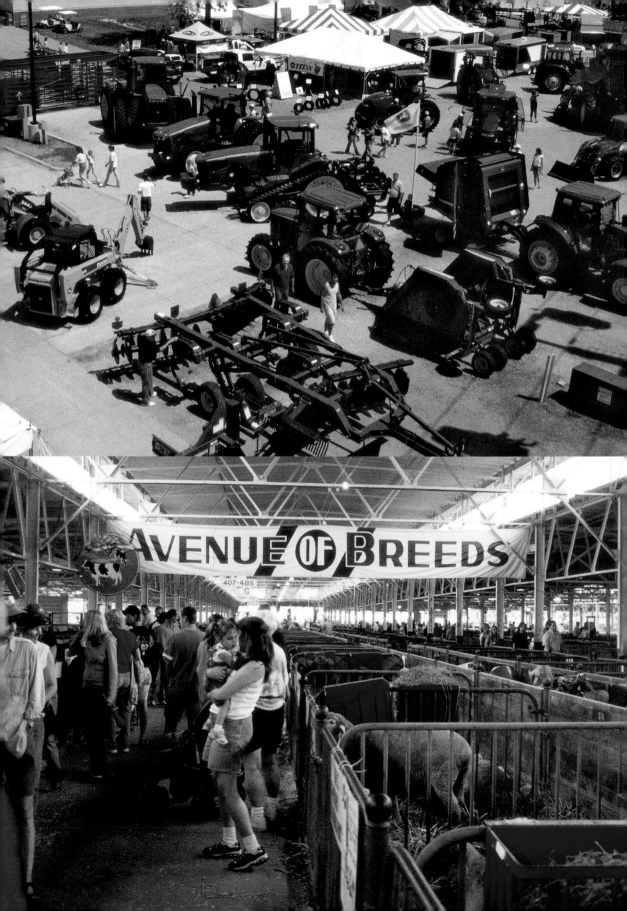

was gradually replaced with a state-of-the-art enclosed exhibition space while preserving the original building frontage along Grand Avenue. This project was the first major building effort on the fairgrounds since the construction of the 4-H dorm (now the Cultural Center) in 1949. Its new materials and clear-span spaces contrasted sharply with the brick and steel of the old barns, and its relationship to the original pavilions serves as a reminder of the gap between past and present. Fairgoers, of course, appreciate the vast, air-conditioned space inside

Agriculture in Iowa and throughout the Midwest has shifted from a family enterprise to one that is heavily industrialized. The demise of the family farm is not quite as imminent as the popular press has claimed, but the national attention occasionally commanded by news of farm woes indicates our ongoing concern about the transition away from our agrarian heritage. The vast majority of farms in Iowa are still owned by families, but pressure to consolidate or to sell is fundamentally changing this population base. Iowa's agricultural population declined in real terms from 1.7 million in 1900 to 1.2 million in 2000.[9] Two-thirds of Iowa's ninety-nine counties lost population over the last century, while its handful of metropolitan areas boomed, attracting residents as financial and manufacturing interests became more important to the state's economy. City dwellers have attended the fair in record numbers, helping to push total attendance over one million in each of the last five years, and their expectations parallel those of the event's urban visitors throughout the twentieth century.

Iowans go to the fair for many reasons: dubious prize-winning opportunities on the Midway; cheesecake on a stick at the fair's food stands; auto races; classic rock in the Grandstand. But these do not explain the hold that the event has on the general public. The unimpeachable nobility of farm life may, ironically, be the fair's greatest attraction to the group of Iowans who rarely get their boots dirty. They marvel at the 4-H competitors who bed down next to their superior livestock, are thrilled to climb into the cabs of combines and tractors, and take in

OPPOSITE

TOP: Agricultural equipment carpets display areas south of the Varied Industries Building.

BOTTOM: The animal barns provide almost exactly the same sights, sounds, and smells as they did a century ago. The Swine Barn is home to 1,100 animals each year, as it has been since its construction.

OPPOSITE
The quiet dignity and
functionality of the animal
barns provides a sober
backdrop for food stalls and
stands of remarkable visual
diversity.

ABOVE
Several classic food stands
have been selling the same
snacks for more than a
generation.

the sounds and smells of what makes the state work, safe in the knowledge that this challenging lifestyle is something they see only once a year. The pleasures of walking through the animal barns are, unquestionably, partly voyeuristic: to see how the other third lives in Iowa. Urban visitors pay for this, whether by stepping in cow pies or falling victim to the time-honored rubber spider dropped from the girders in front of them by a 4-H youth holding its string nearby. But it gives them—gives us—if only for a day, the proud bearing of Iowans dependent on the land and gratification with the results of their hard work.

It is this sense of Midwestern ethics and pragmatism that the fair celebrates, even as Iowa again experiences major shifts in its demographics and economy. Its urban centers have slowly grown more diverse and lively, as its rural areas have aged. Its agricultural economy has changed, as industrialized agriculture has homogenized crops and livestock. The early years of this century have seen an economic boom from the rising importance of ethanol, and some farmers have made the practical choice to replace crops with high-tech windmills; energy is now a major export. Likewise, a new emphasis on organic produce and a burgeoning wine industry have broadened farmers' options and brought back some of the agricultural artisanship and individuality of the fair's early years.

Nevertheless, tensions between tradition and modernity still arise occasionally, as they have throughout the fair's history. In 2002, the "Pickles" debacle highlighted the growing unease among science, tradition, and ethics at the fair. Pickles, a 1,290-pound steer, was named the winning 4-H entry. Later, the fair authority discovered that the blue ribbon winner was—possibly—not the Pickles that had been entered in the competition seven months earlier. Pickles's owner was accused of switching steers, replacing the original entry with one that had grown larger. The subsequent investigation and court case brought unwanted scrutiny to livestock practices in the animal barns.[10] Though rare, instances of cheating are troubling, and the resulting mandate to test

OPPOSITE

TOP: The classic fair lunch—frozen lemonade and a corn dog—is shown here in its final moments.

BOTTOM RIGHT: The Barbeque Cook-off is among the more hotly contested events at the fair, with bragging rights among individuals and restaurants at stake.

BOTTOM LEFT: Iowa barbeque is only complete with a cold mug. The introduction of wine coolers in recent years is a nod to more urbane fairgoers.

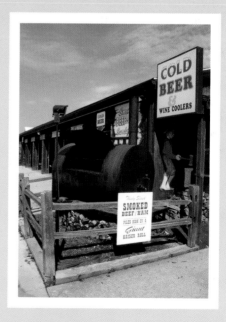

OPPOSITE

TOP AND BOTTOM:
At the fair today, ribbons
are still awarded for
agricultural products,
crafts, and food items.

ABOVE
Textiles and crafts form
a major element in the
fair's competition program,
offering a domestic
counterpart to the
livestock and agricultural
competitions.

DNA to confirm winners' identities has added an uncomfortable layer of technological scrutiny to the 4-H contests.

Such threats to the fair's spirit and traditions are happily remote in the midst of the crowds on a hot August afternoon. Although not immutable, the fair is as close as most get to the mythical agrarian life about which Americans—Midwesterners, in particular—rhapsodize. For over a century, farmers and town folk alike have wandered the animal barns, watched judging in the Livestock Pavilion, were thrilled by racing action in the Grandstand, and dined on fare ranging from barbecued lamb to funnel cakes.[11]

Today, the fairground's highest point is marked by temporary rides offering reverse bungee jumps, Skylon ascents, or high-speed Ferris Wheel-like action. From the parking lots—and even from downtown—the spidery metal arms of these rides offer the first glimpse of the day's activities. And from the summit of these rides, the panorama of the animal barns, the Grandstand, and the crush of one hundred thousand daily attendees is breathtaking. Fairgoers may not recognize that the flat, roughly cruciform land that supports these mega-rides is hallowed ground. But in a neat distillation of the fair's history, the modern visitor, when suspended over the fair on a ride, is immediately above the footprint of William Hackney's long-demolished 1884 Exposition Hall— the fairgrounds' first "permanent" timber structure.

OPPOSITE

TOP: A crowd watches judging in the Sheep Barn in 2005.

BOTTOM: Funnel cakes make a popular, if not balanced, breakfast.

ABOVE

The corn dog is the fair's trademark meal, but it ranks behind other foods— in particular, the pork chop on a stick—in the opinion of experienced fairgoers.

OPPOSITE

TOP LEFT: The 1886 Exposition Building site, now occupied by thrill rides, overlooks the fairgrounds.

TOP RIGHT: Fairgoers take in the best view of the fairgrounds from the Skyride's cable cars.

BOTTOM: Those unwilling to scale the bungee jump towers can still find vertiginous thrills at the Midway.

FROZEN LEMONADE

20 LEMONS
5 QUARTS WATER
5 CUPS SUGAR

Peel lemons and cut into slices.
Sprinkle rinds with sugar and let stand for 1–2 hours.

—

Cover with boiling water, allow to cool, and remove rinds.

—

Squeeze lemon slices into cooled water, stir,
and freeze, stirring every 20 minutes to break up
large chunks of ice.

*This ice-cold treat is even more popular
than beer at the fair,
according to a semi-scientific poll.*

🝆   🝆   🝆

Acknowledgments

This book originated with a paper delivered in a session on rural architecture organized by Christine O'Malley at the Society of Architectural Historians Annual Meeting in 2004. I am grateful to Professor O'Malley for her suggestions and comments on the original paper. Likewise, my fellow panelists at that session—Helen Tangires, Kathy Swift, and Caroline Swope—offered encouragement and suggestions that were crucial in expanding the paper into book form.

Nancy Eklund Later at Princeton Architectural Press made the bold suggestion of turning the paper into this book, and I have appreciated the enthusiasm for butter cows, corn dogs, and hog judging that she has shown over the life of the project.

Sharon Avery at the State Historical Society of Iowa was tireless in providing me with access to the enormous trove of state fair photographs in the society's archives in Des Moines. Lori Cornwell at the Blue Ribbon Foundation provided valuable access to the fairgrounds, both before and during the 2005 fair.

My colleagues in the Department of Architecture at Iowa State shared in the joy of bringing this regional tradition to a wider audience, and I am grateful for their support and enthusiasm. I should note in particular the wisdom of Karen Bermann, who originally wooed us to Iowa with the explicit promise of a "serious state fair"—a promise that has been fulfilled annually.

Finally, this book is dedicated to my fair-going companions, Kathy and our children. Without them I would never have discovered the wonders on a stick that make up the Iowa State Fair.

Notes

INTRODUCTION

1   U.S. Department of Agriculture, from 2000 census.

CHAPTER ONE

1   Myrtle Beinhauer, "The County, District, and State Agricultural Societies of Iowa," *Annals of Iowa* 20, no. 1 (Jul. 1935): 51.

2   "State Agricultural Society," *Iowa Farmer and Horticulturist* 1, no. 2 (Jun. 1853): 22.

3   Beinhauer, "County, District, and State," 55.

4   "List of Premiums for the First Iowa State Fair," *Iowa Farmer and Horticulturist* 1, no. 3 (Jul. 1854): 57.

5   Thomas W. Claggett, letter published in *Iowa Farmer and Horticulturist* I, no. 3 (Jul. 1854): 65. Original spelling retained.

6   Ibid. In the end, the society had to settle for a lecture by a Mr. Dixon of Keokuk, a noted author if only of regional acclaim.

7   Earle D. Ross, "The First Iowa State Fair," *Palimpsest* 35, no. 7 (Jul. 1954): 270.

8   "State Fair at Fairfield," *Iowa Farmer and Horticulturist* II, no. 7 (Nov. 1854): 161.

9   Thomas W. Claggett, letter published in *Iowa Farmer and Horticulturist* II, no. 6 (Oct. 1854).

10 In covering the event, the editors of the *Iowa Farmer* noted that the letter writer had mysteriously been "prevented from even witnessing the triumphant result of her suggestion." The journal's enthusiastic fair boosterism suggests a hidden hand behind this event.

11 "Female Equestrianism at the State Fair," *Iowa Farmer and Horticulturist* II, no. 7 (Nov. 1854): 163.

12 Ibid. 163. See also Beinhauer, "County, District, and State," 58.

13 Former state senator C. J. Fulton of Fairfield noted in 1935 that this popular account did not square with the likely dress of the riders at the time, arguing that contrary to legend the display was "not a circus." He contended that the riders "rode modestly on sidesaddles as they were accustomed to ride." C. J. Fulton, letter to the editor, published in *The Annals of Iowa* 20, no. 2 (Oct. 1935): 151–52.

14 Ross, "First Iowa State Fair," 279.

15 Premium List for the State Fair at Dubuque, Iowa (Dubuque: Iowa State Agricultural Society, 1863). Source Iowa State University Library Collections.

16 Premium List for the State Fair at Burlington, Iowa (Burlington: Iowa State Agricultural Society, 1865). Source Iowa State University Library Collections.

17 "Source Material of Iowa History: The Iowa State Fair of 1856," *Iowa Journal of History* 54, no. 2 (Apr. 1956): 169–84. [Reprint of Report of the Society, 1857.]

CHAPTER TWO

1   William J. Petersen, *The Story of Iowa: The Progress of an American State* (New York: Lewis Historical Publishing Co., 1952), 586.

2   "Only One Week More," *Iowa State Register*, 27 Aug. 1886 (morning ed.).

3   *Iowa State Register*, 29 Aug. 1886.

4   Ibid.

5   R. C. Webb, in charge of stands, amusements, and food stalls, declared: "I have already sold three or four thousand dollars worth of space for amusement stands, side-shows, eating houses and such affairs. I have sold about fifteen spaces for eating houses, and will sell fifteen or twenty more before the fair. They will all be needed to supply the people with food. Five or six side shows have been engaged, some of them being first class exhibitions. We will have the famous picture of the Battle of Gettysburg on the grounds, and Cohen's big show from Chicago, with a varied collection of curiosities and art works, has taken out a license.... There will be plenty of chance for everyone to be amused and fed and instructed.... The management will not allow the sale of any kind of prohibited liquors on the grounds, and are guarding carefully the character of all shows and amusements admitted." "The Coming Fair." *Iowa State Register*, 29 Aug. 1886.

6   Myrtle Beinhauer, "The County, District, and State Agricultural Societies of Iowa," *Annals of Iowa* 20, no. 1 (Jul. 1935): 63–64.

7   *Iowa Homestead*, 7 Feb. 1890.

8   Like the Ak-Sar-Ben society of Omaha, Nebraska, "Seni-Om-Sed" partook of the era's odd fascination with mysterious—though easily decoded—names.

9   Iowa Homestead, 31 Aug., 1894. Pg. 8.

10 "The state of Iowa cannot afford to have a fair that builds up the agricultural industries of the state and which is as conspicuous for its moral tone as it is for its display of farm products headed in the direction of the fast horse as its crowning and culminating feature. It cannot afford to drive away from it the sober, staid but clear-headed and conscientious farmers who strive to curb and crush out the gambling spirit, and invite the accessories and concomitants of the horse race.... The morals of the state cannot be sacrificed to pour money into Des Moines, even if the *Register* is willing and anxious for it." *Iowa Homestead*, 5 Sept. 1890.

11 "Record Yet Unbroken," *Des Moines Leader*, 9 Sept. 1896.

12 *Des Moines Leader*, 14 Apr. 1898.

13 Beinhauer, "County, District, and State Agricultural Societies," 64.

14 "People Pouring into City," *Des Moines Leader*, 25 Aug. 1901; "The State Fair A Success," *Iowa State Register*, 27 Aug. 1901.

15 "What the State Fair Needs," *Iowa State Register*, 25 Aug. 1901.

16 "Des Moines' Greatest Industry" and "Paving and Building Brick," advert., *Iowa State Register*, 25 Aug. 1901, 10, 12–13.

17 "Fair Will Clear $10,000," *Iowa State Register*, 30 Aug. 1901.

18 "Improve the State Fair," *Iowa State Register*, 30 Aug. 1901.

19 "Fair Ground Improvement," *Iowa State Register*, 1 Sept. 1901.

20 Ibid.

21 "To Be Greatest Iowa State Fair," *Iowa State Register*, 17 Aug. 1902.

22 "Everything Now Is in Readiness," *Iowa State Register*, 22 Aug. 1902.

23 "A Twentieth Century Fair." *Iowa State Register*, 20 Aug. 1902.

24 "Fair Surplus of $15,000 in Sight," *Iowa State Register*, 29 Aug. 1902.

25 "Big Fair Ends with a Surplus in the Strong Box," *Des Moines Register and Leader*, 31 Aug. 1907; "Big Changes Made at Fair Grounds," *Des Moines Register and Leader*, 21 Aug. 1909.

26 "Liberati Charms Large Audiences," *Des Moines Register and Leader*, 30 Aug. 1909.

27 Iowa State Fair: Historical Highlights, pamphlet (Des Moines: Iowa State Fair, 1983).

28 "Fair Visitors Witness Novel Plowing Race," *Des Moines Register and Leader*, 25 Aug. 1907.

CHAPTER THREE

1 "Speed Work on Buildings for the Fair," *Des Moines Register,* 18 Aug. 1927.

2 "Veteran's Day Lure Throngs to State fair," *Des Moines Register,* 28 Aug. 1927.

3 "Lindy Arrives Amid Cheer of Thousands," *Des Moines Register,* 30 Aug. 1927.

4 "Iowa State Fair: Historical Highlights" (Des Moines: Iowa State Fair, 1983).

5 Earle D. Ross, "A Dynamic Quarter Century," *Palimpsest* XXXV, no. 7 (Jul. 1954): 309.

6 Ibid.

7 Chris Allen Rasmussen, "State Fair: Culture and Agriculture in Iowa, 1854–1941" (Dissertation, Rutgers University, 1992) provides the most thorough interpretation of Stong's book, along with the most complete social history of the fair to that point.

8 "Iowa: It's Not Art," *Newsweek*, 15 Jul. 1946, 31.

9 Iowa State Fair Board, "Report of the 1946 Iowa State Fair" (Des Moines: State of Iowa, 1946), 4–5.

10 *Wallace's Farmer*, quoted in ibid., 13–15.

11 Iowa State Fair Annual Reports, 1946–50. Iowa State University Library Collections.

12 Photographs in the collection of the State Historical Society of Iowa.

13 "Iowa Farm and Home Register," *Des Moines Sunday Register*, 22 Aug. 1954.

14 "Iowa: It's Not Art."

15 Ibid.

16 *Des Moines Register*, 18 Jan. 1950.

CHAPTER FOUR

1 Mary Kay Shanley, *Our State Fair: Iowa's Blue Ribbon Story* (Ames, Iowa: Iowa State Fair Blue Ribbon Foundation, 2000), 252–55.

2 Photographs in the Iowa State Fair Authority Collection, Photo Archives, State Historical Society of Iowa.

3 A typical description, from 1961, reads: "Johnny Puleo and his Harmonica Gang—"Live and lively! Two-hour, star-studded spectacular. Top stars of stage, nightclub, TV, headline a huge cast of over 200. Gorgeous costumes, lovely dancing chorus, breathtaking settings. Thrill to great music, scintillating songs, bright comedy, lavish production numbers. Unforgettable evenings of pure enchantment under the stars." Advertisement, *Wallace's Farmer*, 19 Aug. 1961. That year the fair also featured a tribute to the Civil War centennial and special exhibits

on nuclear energy entitled "You and the Atom," sponsored by the U.S. Atomic Energy Commission.

4   Various advertisements in *Wallace's Farmer* for the Iowa State Fair, 1965–75. Liberace starred in perhaps the most unusual spectacle at the Grandstand in 1969, demanding some explanation from the organizers: "Liberace, a concert pianist, made himself a bizarre legend with an oversized grand piano, insured for $150,000, and extravagantly sequined tuxedos." *Wallace's Farmer*, 9 Aug. 1969.

5   Advertisement, "1964 Iowa State Fair," *Wallace's Farmer*, 15 Aug. 1964.

6   Ms. Lyon has more recently sculpted figures ranging from a Harley-Davidson motorcycle to a life-size replica of Leonardo's "Last Supper." The use of agricultural products to create sculptures is a long-standing fair tradition, although changing attitudes toward cooking doomed the Pork Producers' annual Lard Pig in the early 1980s.

7   "A Proud Iowa Tradition Crumbles in Distress," pamphlet (Des Moines, Iowa: Iowa State Fair Foundation, 1989).

8   In 1996, a popular ride at the intersection of the Midway and Grand Avenue, Ye Old Mill, collapsed in an off-season windstorm. The dark, tunneled flume ride that had inspired countless teen romances and not a few Iowa marriages was quickly rebuilt.

9   U.S. Bureau of the Census figures, as prepared by the State Library of Iowa.

10   Jerry Perkins, Farm Editor for the *Des Moines Register*, interviewed by Renee Montaigne, NPR News. NPR Morning Edition, National Public Radio, 6 Aug. 2003.

11   The lamb marketing board has for some years placed its barbeque stand disconcertingly adjacent to the Sheep Barn's entry, although this seems not to have fazed true Lamburger connoisseurs.

Bibliography

Beinhauer, Myrtle. "The County, District, and State Agricultural Societies of Iowa." *Annals of Iowa* 20, no. 1 (Jul. 1935): 50–69.

Des Moines Register and Leader/Des Moines Register. Des Moines, Iowa: Des Moines Register and Tribune Co., ff. 1860.

Economic Research Associates. *Long Range Planning for the Iowa State Fair and World Food Exposition.* Los Angeles: Economic Research Associates, 1968.

"Huh-ry! Huh-ry! Iowa State Fair." *Newsweek* 42 (14 Sept. 1953): 36.

"I Sing of America: Iowa State Fair." *Holiday* 56 (Mar. 1975): 37.

"Iowa Farm and Home Register." *Des Moines Sunday Register*, 22 Aug. 1954. [Special issue on the fair's centennial.]

Iowa Farmer and Horticulturist. Burlington, Iowa, 1853–60.

"Iowa State Fair." *Christian Science Monitor Magazine*, 1 Sept. 1937, 4.

Iowa State Fair: Historical Highlights. Des Moines: Iowa State Fair, 1983.

Iowa State Fair Board. Annual Reports of the Iowa State Fair. Des Moines: State of Iowa, 1946–present.

"Iowa's State Fair." *Holiday* 39 (May 1966).

Mahan, Bruce E. "The Seventh Iowa State Fair." *Palimpsest*, Oct. 1926, 309–20.

"Mecca along the Midway." *Time* 102 (10 Sept. 1973): 27.

"National Affairs: It's Not Art." *Newsweek* 28 (15 July 1946): 31.

Neely, Wayne Caldwell. *The Agricultural Fair.* New York: Columbia University Press, 1935.

Petersen, William J. *The Story of Iowa: The Progress of an American State.* New York: Lewis Historical Publishing Co., 1952.

Premium Lists of the State Fair at Des Moines, Iowa. Des Moines: Iowa State Agricultural Society, 1857–present.

"A Proud Iowa Tradition Crumbles in Distress." Des Moines: Iowa State Fair Foundation, 1989.

Rasmussen, Chris Allen. "State Fair: Culture and Agriculture in Iowa, 1854–1941." Ph.D. dissertation, Rutgers University, 1992.

Ross, Earle D. "The First Iowa State Fair." *Palimpsest* 35, no. 7 (Jul. 1954): 261–325.

"Rural Revelry." *Time* 26 (9 Sept. 1935): 12–16.

Shanley, Mary Kay. *Our State Fair: Iowa's Blue Ribbon Story.* Des Moines: Iowa State Fair Blue Ribbon Foundation, 2000.

"Source Material of Iowa History: The Iowa State Fair of 1856." *Iowa Journal of History* 154, no. 2 (Apr. 1956): 169–84. [Reprint of Report of the Society, 1857.]

"State Fair Art, Indigenous Fertility." *American Magazine of Art* 26 (Oct. 1933): 476–78.

Wallace's Farmer. Des Moines, Iowa: Wallace-Homestead Co., 1893–present.